FAVORITE PLACES

to go with kids in

ST. LOUIS

A Guide to Children's Activities
in Greater St. Louis

By Ann Seebeck

Photographs by Ann Seebeck

ISBN 0-9622044-04
Library of Congress Catalog Card Number 89-90834
Hi/tec Copy Center
375 N. Big Bend Blvd. • St. Louis, MO 63130
design@hiteccopy.com • (314) 863-4111

PREFACE

This booklet was written to fulfill my own needs when I took my children to places of interest in the Greater St. Louis area. I had been keeping a file of favorite places to go with kids in St. Louis and after sharing the file with several friends it was suggested that I put the file into booklet form. This is not meant to be a complete guide, but rather to point out some of my favorite places to go with kids in St. Louis. It is basically for preschool, kindergarten, and grade school age children, with a few new additions for older children, however, the entire family will enjoy many of these experiences.

I have tried to suggest a balance of recreational, cultural, and historical activities, but the main emphasis is HAVING FUN with your children. My family, friends, and I have had an enjoyable summer visiting these places.

I am constantly updating this book but I would suggest that you recheck the hours and prices as they are all subject to change.

At the end of each section there is a blank page for you to add some of your favorite places.

If you have any suggestions or new ideas to add to this book, please let me know.

Ann Seebeck
July 2012

Ann Seebeck
1018 Edgeworth
Kirkwood, MO 63122

*To my loving husband, Rick;
to my wonderful son Tim;
to my son Chris, who is at
peace in heaven but will
always be in my heart; and
to my great family and friends
who help me in so many ways.*

TABLE OF CONTENTS

Museums & Entertainment

MUSEUMS AND ENTERTAINMENT

Mississippi Riverfront

1. ***Gateway Arch*** – On the Mississippi Riverfront, downtown. 655-1700. Open 8:00 am. - 9:30 pm. Winter hours are 9:00 am. - 6:00 pm.(Last Tram ride leaves 50 mins. before closing) Tram rides to the top of the Arch are $10.00 adults, $5.00 for children 3 to 15 years old; which includes the $3.00 entrance fee. You can purchase tickets in advance. There are price breaks for adding any 3 of the movies. Also there is a Museum of Westward Expansion underneath Arch. Lots of fun things to look at: Indian teepee, covered wagon, sod house, Lewis and Clark Expedition; preserved animals such as a bear, buffalo, beavers and appaloosa horse, tools of the miners and explorers all depicting the hardships of the people traveling west in the 1800s. National Park Rangers provide frequent and free talks on the exhibits. Group and school tours are available. Large park and picnic area on the grounds of the arch. Beneath the Arch is a new 4-story-high movie theater with shows every 45 mins. The movies now showing are Monument of a Dream and The Great American West.

2. ***Becky Thatcher and Tom Sawyer Riverboat Ride*** – Mississippi riverfront, downtown. 621-4040. 1 hour rides up and down the river starting at 10:30 am., leaving every 1 1/2 hours until 4:30 p.m., weather permitting. Times may vary for different seasons. Snack bar on board with sodas and hot dogs. Adults $14.00, children 12 to 3 $8.00 and under 3 free. Call first to check on the times because they can vary. Arrive at least 15 mins. earlier than departing time.

3. ***Raging Rivers Waterpark*** – Grafton, Illinois (along the Great River Rd.) (618) 786-2345. Take I-270 North to 367, to Alton, IL, to IL Highway 100 in Grafton (Great River Rd.) Go about 14 miles north. This is a fun waterpark with 5 different water activities including Itty Bitty Surf City, just for the small children. You could spend the day here just relaxing on the Lazy River ride, or bouncing with excitement on the flume ride or giant wave pool. There is a concession stand with lots of umbrella tables (no coolers allowed) and picnic tables outside in the parking lot. There are lockers, showers, and a gift shop. Adults are $20.95 and children 3 to 8 years are $17.95. After 3 pm. daily, save $5.00 off regular price. There is a $5.00 parking fee. There is an extra tube rental for some rides of $4.00 for a single tube and $6.00 for a double tube. Hours are 10:30 am to 6:00 pm.

Downtown

4. **City Museum** – 701 N. 15th Street. downtown. The International Arts Complex. 231-CITY. This is a wonderful new museum. It is "part of the heartbeat of the city." This is a group of independently operated museums and hands-on activities and displays all under one big roof! There is The Glass Studio, which will demonstrate glass blowing and other glass art, an Architectural Museum which has treasures from many parts of St. Louis, a model train that you can ride, everyday circus has live entertainment and carnival games, the Museum of Mirth, Mystery & Mayhem has exhibits as seen in a carnival midway, and many, many more. The first floor is like a fantasy land created by sculptor Robert Cassilly (of Turtle Park fame). You can walk right into the mouth of a life size whale, or you can wonder among the root systems of a tree or climb in a birds nest. You can go inside a cave or watch the fish in the 35,000 gallon fish tank! You can see an 1800's log cabin or you can nibble on a sandwich upstairs at the Café. This museum is also the ultimate in recycling since many of its displays and art work are a creative re-use of materials. On the second floor is The World Aquarium with its unique hands-on exhibits and "touch pools" where you can pet a shark, a turtle and many creatures. There is a large shark tank, a stingray pool, squid, crabs, and star fish. A great place to explore and learn. There is a separate admission to the Aquarium of $6.00 per person in addition to the City Museum admission. City Museum admission is $12.00 per person, ages 36 months and up. After 5 pm on Fri. and Sat. nights admission is $10.00 per person. Group rates available for both City Museum and World Aquarium. City Museum hours are Sunday 11:00 am - 5:00 pm; (Summer, Memorial Day - Labor Day, Monday and Tuesday 9:00 am - 5:00 pm) Closed Monday and Tues. in the winter. Wednesday - Thursday 9:00 am - 5:00 pm; Friday 9:00 am - 1:00 am; Saturday 10:00 am - 1:00 am.

5. **Tram Tours** – 241-1400- Tour St. Louis by tram or van. What a nice way to see the city without the hassles of parking or walking too far. Learn the little known secrets of St. Louis by expert guides. All day tours are $45.00, half day tours are $35.00, and children under 5 yrs. are free. There is also a special family price. Group prices are available too. Call for reservations.

6. **Metro Link** – 231-2345 – Lightrail system in St. Louis. Even if you don't have a destination in mind it is fun to just ride the rail! You can park and ride at the North Hanley Rd. and I-70 Station near the air-

port and go passed University of Missouri, Delmar Loop, Forest Park, Central west end, Union Station, Busch Stadium, the convention center, Laclede's Landing, and just across the Mississippi River, and back again. Rides are $2.50 each way for adults, and $1.50 for children. Trains leave each station every few mins. Be sure you validate your ticket for each way you travel. Transfers to buses are available at each stop.

7. **Old Court House** – 11 North 4th St., downtown. 655-1700. Open daily 8:00 am. to 4:30 pm. For the older children this is interesting. There are restored court rooms and museum galleries about the history of St. Louis. School groups in the 4th grade and up can participate in a mock trial in the old courtrooms, complete with costumes and scripts. The Dred Scott trial is a favorite because it happened right there.

8. **Dental Health Theatre** – 727 N. 1st. St., downtown. 241-7391 - Hours 9:00 am. - 3:00 pm. Wednesday-Saturday. Call for reservations. $1.00 per person. Demonstrations with 16 three-foot high fiberglass teeth; films and puppet shows on dental health care. This theatre is the only one of its kind in the world!

9. **Bob Kramer's Marionettes** – 4143 Laclede Ave., downtown. 531-3313. Take Highway 40 east to Kingshighway north to Forest Park Parkway east. Go left on Sarah to Laclede. Turn left and it is 1/2 block down on Laclede. You can see how marionettes are made, the history of puppetry and a puppet show. A studio demonstration and puppet show together begin at 10:00 a.m. Monday – Saturday and 1:00 p.m. on Sunday. It is $12.00 for adults and $10.00 for children. Reservations are required.

10. **Eugene Field House and Toy Museum** – 634 S. Broadway, downtown. 421-4689. Closed Monday and Tuesday. Open Wed. - Sat., 10:00 am. - 4:00 pm. Sun. 12:00 pm. - 4:00 pm. Admission: adults $5.00, children 11 years and younger $1.00, under 3 years is free. This is the house where the poet Eugene Field grew up. (His works include "Little Boy Blue" and "Wynken, Blynken, and Nod"). The house is furnished with personal treasures, furniture and antique toys belonging to the Field family.

11. **Soulard Farmer's Market**– Corner of 7th St. and Lafayette Ave. 622-4180.This Farmer's market is one of the oldest public markets in the United States. Take the kids shopping for fresh fruits, vegetables,

fish, flowers, and many others! It is an experience to remember. Open Wed. - Sat. 8 am to 5 pm.

12. **Busch Stadium** – 420 S. 8th St., St. Louis, 345-9600. The new stadium is wonderful! Everyone loves the St. Louis Cardinals! Check a schedule for days and times the Cardinals are in town. Kids can even get a Build-a-Bear Fred Bird!

13. **The Dome** – Broadway at Convention Plaza, Downtown St. Louis. 342-5000. This is the home of the St. Louis Rams football team. St. Louis fought very hard to get this stadium and its football team; let's cheer them on!

14. **Cahokia Mounds Historic Site and Museum** – 7850 Collinsville Rd., Collinsville, Il. Along I-55 and I-70. 618-346-5160. The remains of the largest prehistoric city north of Mexico. The museum has many artifacts dating back to 700 A.D., dioramas, slide show, and a mirrored village of the sites. See the sun calendar called Woodhenge and climb 100 feet to the top of Monks Mound for a spectacular view of the area. Many special events throughout the year. Call for dates. Open 9 to 5 p.m. daily. Admission is free, but they do take donations.

Forest Park

15. **St. Louis Zoo** – Forest Park, 781-0900. Summer hours are 8:00 a.m. to 7 p.m. daily. Winter hours are 9:00 a.m. to 5:00 p.m. daily. Entrance is free. Parking is $15.00. Every part of the zoo is fun! And most of the animal exhibits are free! See Raja and all the other elephants, hippos and other animals in the River's Edge. See the Penguin and Puffin Coast and watch them swim and play. There is a carousel that you can ride on the backs of the different protected and endangered animals. This is $3.00 a ticket. See Big Cat Country, The Fragile Forest, and the 1904 World's Fair walk-through birdcage. Take a ride on the Zoo Railroad Train and get a good overall view of the zoo. You can get off at different stations to see the animals or you can ride all the way around. Tickets are $5.00 a person. In the Children's Zoo section you can feed the goats and lorikeet birds, learn about the animals in the amphitheater, play on the outdoor equipment and swim with the otters! Yes, you can slide through a see-through tube that goes into the otter pool and not even get wet! If you prefer to get wet, you can run through the water geysers. The Children's Zoo is $4.00 a person. Pet the stingrays at Caribbean Cove, May – September. $3.00 per person. Sea Lion shows are several times a

day at $4.00 a person. The new Sea Lion Sound has a walk-through tunnel where you can view the sea lions underwater. In the summer from 8:00 a.m. to 9:00 a.m. the Children's Zoo and the carousel are free. In the winter they are free from 9:00 a.m. to 10:00 a.m. The Lakeside Café and the Painted Giraffe Restaurant have both indoor and outdoor seating and a children's lunch speical. The Educational Center, called The Living World, has two special display rooms. one is Amphibians and has many tad poles, frogs, fish, snakes, newts and more. The other room is called Zoomagination Station and is a discovery room where the smaller children can explore and discover in many shelves, drawers and tables full of intersting new things. This is open Wed. – Sun. 10 am. to 4 pm. in 45 min sessions. This building is free and has a restaurant and gift shop. Strollers are available for rent. Birthday parties are also available at the zoo. See Birthday Parties chapter.

16. *Art Museum* – Forest Park- 721-0067. Closed Monday. Open Tue. - Sun. 10:00 a.m. - 5:00 p.m., Fri. 10:00 a.m. – 9:00 p.m. The Museum is nice place for a quiet walk and an introduction to a variety of art objects. Check with museums calendar for any special exhibits and children's art classes. There are several Family Days throughout the year. Kids love to visit the Mummy and see the x-ray of his bones. Special exhibits are free on Fridays.

17. *Jefferson Memorial or Missouri Historical Society or Missouri History Museum* – Forest Park- 746-4599. Open daily 10:00 am to 6:00 pm; Tuesday until 8:00 pm. The wonderful addition to this museum tells about the past, present and future of Missouri. Exhibits are first-class, interesting and educational. There are a lot of hands-on exhibits for the kids to explore. There is a restaurant, snack bar, and gift shop. Some fun and different things for kids to look at: antique toys, Charles Lindbergh memorabilia, exhibits on life in early St. Louis, and a special 1904 World's Fair exhibit. They have many special programs designed for children throughout the year. For any special exhibits that require a ticket, they can be seen free to St. Louis City and County residents on Tues. from 2:00 – 8:00 p.m.

18. *St. Louis Science Center* – Forest Park and 5050 Oakland Ave. 289-4444. Parking on the Oakland lot is $10.00 (members of the Science Center park free). Museum hours are Mon. – Thurs. 9:30 am – 4:30 pm, Fri. 9:30 am – 9:30 pm, Sat. 9:30 am – 4:30 pm, Sun. 11:30 am – 4:30 pm. Hours are subject to change. Admission: Free. The Science Center is spectacular! A must for all to see.

There are many hands-on learning exhibits, life-size moving dinosaurs, computers to work, exhibits on ecology and the environment, radar guns in the walkway above the highway, the Discovery Room, and a 4-story-high theater. The Omnimax Theater (a 40 min. show) has shows daily. Call for today's schedule. Admission: $9.00 adults and $8.00 for children or seniors. The Discovery Room, a hands-on room for the younger ones, is $3.50 per person. You should make reservations and purchase tickets for any of these shows upon entering the Science Center. A snack bar and gift shop are in the Center. The Planetarium has a whole new look. When you enter the lower level, it looks like a futuristic airport. Blast off to the space station and enjoy many hands-on exhibits. Experience over 9,000 stars projected on the dome of the Planetarium and learn about many of them. Admission to the Planetarium's Space Station Experience is $5.00 adults, $4.00 children and seniors. Call for entry times.

19. **Forest Park Boathouse** – 367-2224. Enjoy the wonderful new boathouse! Paddleboats amd rowboats are available for rental at $15 per hour/$3 every 15 min. there after. Mon. – Sun. 10 am. to sunset; In the fall and winter, Sunday is 11am. to sunset. You can paddle around the lake, under bridges and to the Grand Basin in front of the Art Museum. Great fun! There is also a great restaurant which serves lunch, dinner and Sunday brunch. Indoor seating or enjoy patio seating along the dock.

City of St. Louis

20. **Missouri Botanical Gardens** – 4344 Shaw. 577-5100. Open daily 9:00 am -. 5:00 pm. Memorial Day - Labor Day it has extended hours on Wed. until 8:00 pm. Non St. Louis City or County residents, adults are $8.00, children 12 years and under free. St. Louis City and County residents, adults are $4.00, children under 12 are free. St. Louis City and County residents are free Wed. and Sat. mornings, 9:00 am to noon; and during the summer, Wed. evenings 5:00 pm. to 8:00 pm. Nice relaxing place for a walk. Japanese Garden walk is beautiful (bring quarters for food to feed the hundreds of Carp fish in the lake). Let your children try their skills through the Kaeser Maze; a maze of yew bushes they can wander through. Cafeteria style restaurant, good salads and sandwiches, and hot dogs for the kids. Watch the paper for special children's events throughout the year, which include a storytelling day, a plant day, and of course the special summer Japanese Festival and for the holidays see the miniature train and flower display in the Gardenland Express. Visit the

Climatron, its notable features are waterfalls and beautiful tropical plants. Now open is the Doris Schnuck Children's Garden called "A Missouri Adventure," which is an interactive look at Missouri in the 1800's. $3.00 for member's children 3-12 years old and $5.00 for non-members. Adults free.

21. ***Prologue Room*** – Boeing Building 100 at McDonnell Blvd. and Airport Rd., adjacent to Lambert St. Louis International Airport. Enter at Gate 101. 232-6896. This special display room is open during the summer months, from the day after Memorial Day to the Friday before Labor Day. Hours are 9:00 am. to 4:00 pm Monday through Friday. This exhibit shows the history of flight with models from the earliest planes to life size space capsules. Very interesting to the older kids. Free admission. Reservations required.

22. ***BigFoot Truck*** – 6311 N. Lindbergh. 731-2822. (Lindbergh past I-270, past Boeing Co., and across from the Ford Plant. Turn left on Utz Rd. and right on Brooks Rd.) This is a BIG truck in a fenced in parking lot. You can walk all around and under this truck and even stand up inside its wheels! The little kids love it. It's really the place where they make BigFoot Trucks and at certain times you can look out a glass room and watch them work. Inside the store are some small Bigfoots the kids can play in, plus videos of Bigfoots and some gifts. You can also have a birthday party here. Hours are Mon. - Fri. 9:00 am to 5:00 pm. and Sat. 9:00 am. to 1:00 pm. Free.

23. ***St. Louis Walk of Fame*** – 6504 Delmar, St. Louis/University City/ The Loop area, (314) 727-STAR. The Walk of Fame consists of 100's of sets of brass stars and bronze plaques set into the sidewalks of the 6200–6600 blocks of Delmar Blvd. in the exciting shopping/restaurant/ entertainment/arts district called "The Loop." These stars honor famous St. Louisans and the plaques briefly summarize their achievements and their St. Louis connections, making this walk enjoyable and educational. Some of the stars include John Goodman, Maya Angelou, Bob Costas, Miles Davis, Chuck Berry, Tennessee Williams, Stan Musial, Tina Turner, Charles Lindbergh, T.S. Eliot, Scott Joplin, Yogi Berra and Betty Grable. Many teachers bring their students here on field trips to make chalk rubbings of the stars and plaques and then back at school the children give reports about great St. Louisans who have had a national impact on our cultural heritage. The Walk of Fame is free of charge and open all year. Along these blocks there are several places to stop for refreshments, including Blueberry Hill Restaurant, which has a large collection of pop culture memorabilia and pictures of famous stars.

South St. Louis

24. **Grants Farm** – 10501 Gravois. 843-1700. Season: Mid-April to end of Oct. Closed Mondays except for a few holidays. Call for hours because they vary with the season, but generally entrance is from 9:00 am - 3:00 pm. Admission is free. Parking is $12.00. The last tram leaves the station a few hours before closing. In the summer it is best to get there early before it gets too crowded or the animals that you can feed get too full! This is a very fun place to go! You ride a tram to the main part of the farm, but first your tram passes a cabin built by Ulysses S. Grant, and travels through 160 acres of open land where over 100 kind of animals roam. When your tram arrives at the main farm area you get off and see the rest by walking at your leisure. You can see the famous Clydesdale horses, monkeys, turtles, bears, kangaroos, pigs, and even bottle-feed the goats. (Bring $1.00!) There is a free bird show and also a carousel ride for $2.00. There are several refreshment areas, with lots of hot dogs, soda, and a free beer for the adults! Visit the stable area and see more horses and a collection of carriages. When you are done, you board the tram again and it will take you back to the entrance. Next to the parking lot, be sure to visit the **Ulysses S. Grant National Historic Site**. Free.

25. **Tower Tee Batting Range** – 6727 Heege Rd., between Laclede Station and MacKenzie Rd. 752-7767. Open between March 1 and October 31. Hours are 9 a.m. to 10 p.m. Sat. and Sun., and 10 a.m. to 10 p.m. Mon. - Fri. A great place to go to get in shape for the ball season! There are 9 pitching machines, some for baseball, some for softball, and fast pitch. 3 games of 15 pitches for $1.00 or team rates (group of 6 or more) for $28 for 1 hour (team rates would be great for birthdays, too!). There is also an 18 hole miniature golf course for $3.00, a driving range, and for the beginner softball players, a sponge ball pitching machine! Soda and Snowcones are available.

26. **Chuck E. Cheese's** – Pizza Parlor where the kids come first! Good pizza, animated stage show, lots of games, and rides. It is dinner and the nights entertainment all in one place. The kids love it! (But it is noisy!). They also do Birthday Parties.

- 720 South County Center Way - (314) 487-7317

- 2669 Bogey Rd. St.Charles- (636) 946-3444

- 15913 Manchester Rd., Ellisville - (636) 391-2391

West County and North County

27. *Magic House* – 516 Kirkwood Rd.- 822-8900. Admission is $8.75 per person. Group rates are available. Summer hours, after Memorial Day, 9:30 am. - 5:30 pm. Mon. - Thurs.; 9:30 am. - 9:00 pm. Fri., 9:30 am. - 5:30 pm. Sat.; 11:30 am. - 5:30 pm. Sun. Call for Winter hours. The Magic House has expanded to over twice its size with twice as much fun! Lots of the favorite hands-on exhibits are still there including the Children's Village, where you can pretend to work in a bank, grocery store, TV station or on a construction site. There is a Star-Spangled Center which features the US President's Oval Office, a court room, and a legislative chamber. There are also large musical instruments the kids can touch and play. Kids can play detective and solve mysteries, and also look at finger prints and shoe tracks. There is even a Picnic Basket Café. There is a special section For Baby and Me just for infants, toddlers and their parents where they can play in a boat or in a peek-a-boo house and hear nursery rhymes and songs. The Magic House is fun for the whole family and can be enjoyed over and over again. Every 3rd Friday of the month from 5:30 pm to 9:00 pm is FREE for parents and up to 4 of their own children.

28. *Painted Zebra* – 10907 Manchester Rd., Kirkwood. 965-2262. This is a new concept in entertainment that is popping up all over the place. It is designing and painting ceramic bisque ware from their stock. They supply the workplace, paint, brushes, glaze, stencils, idea book, and even clean up the mess! When you are finished, they fire your piece for you in their kiln and you can pick it up in a few days. Prices for bisque range from $3.00 to $30.00. Paint time is $7.00 per person. It's a great way to spend time with a friend and get gifts made at the same time! You can even have adult parties or children's birthday parties here. Children's parties are $5.00 per person plus the price of each bisque ware they pick. Open 7 days a week; Mon. - Fri. 11 a.m. to 8 p.m., Sat. 10 a.m. to 8 p.m., Sun. 12 noon to 5 p.m.

29. *Gateway Music Together* – Many locations in St. Louis. (314) 603-7464. You can sign up for classes with your child, infants to Kindergartners, to sing and dance together. Music is learned together though the developmentally appropriate activities including songs, instrument play, rhythm chants and movement. Check out the website; www.GatewayMusicTogether.com

30. *Amtrak Train Ride* – Kirkwood to Downtown and back. 1-800-872-7245. Kirkwood station- (314) 984-8617. Ride the Amtrak train

from the Kirkwood station 12:53 p.m. daily and arrive at St. Louis Amtrak Station - 430 S. 15th St. at 1:35 p.m. You can walk 3 blocks over to Union Station Plaza at 18th and Market, and spend 1 hour shopping around and finding great snacks! Then at 3:30 p.m. catch Amtrak back to Kirkwood and arrive around 3:50 p.m. Adults $14.00 round trip and children 2 to 15 years are half price. Hours and prices can vary. Kids love to ride the train and walk up and down exploring the train. There is usually a snack bar dining car. The Kirkwood Station is not staffed with ticket agents right now. You can buy tickets online, through a travel agent, go to the St. Louis station and buy them, or pay cash when you board the train.

31. ***Museum of Transportation*** – 3015 Barrett Station Rd. 965-7998. Summer hours (Memorial Day - Labor Day) Mon. - Sat. 9:00 am - 5:00 pm; Sun. 11:00 am - 5:00 pm. Winter hours are Tues. - Sat. 9:00 am - 5:00 pm; Sunday 11:00 am –4:00 pm. Adults $8.00; children 3 to 12 yrs. and Seniors $5.00; and under 3 are free. This is a very large area filled with many kinds of transportation including trains, trolleys, cars, buses, boats, and airplanes. You can climb onto many old trains and look around and even ring the bell! There is also a miniature train you can ride on around the property for $4.00. The Automotive building is rebuilt and holds many classic cars. There is also a new Creation Station for the young ones with lots of hands-on activities including Thomas the Tank Engine trains. There is a $2.00 fee. Individual tours and group tours are available. Birthday parties are available in the Creation Station, or an outdoor guided tour party. Call (314) 289-3508 for reservations. Also visit the Museum of Transport's exhibits on the second level of Union Station Plaza, Downtown, called the Memories Museum. It has model trains, photos, and memorabilia when Union Station was a busy train station. Free and open during regular mall hours. They also have a gift shop on the first level.

32. ***Craft Caboose*** – 105 East Argonne Ave., Kirkwood (314) 835-9977. This is a great arts and crafts studio just for kids! Crafts are age appropriate for kids around ages 2 to 6 years old. You can attend by going to classes, parties, play dates, or walk-ins. Hours are 9:30 a.m. – 5:00 p.m. Tues. - Sat. *(Closed Monday)* Closed Sunday, except for booked parties.

33. ***Puzzle Warehouse*** – 655 Leffingwell Ave., Kirkwood (314) 856-4030. (I-44 to Big Bend to Holmes to Leffingwell) This is the biggest puzzle store I have ever seen; over 12,000 puzzles for every age

group and puzzle difficulty. Hours are Mon. – Fri. 9 a.m.- 8:00 p.m.; Sat. 9:00 a.m.- 6:00 p.m.; Sun. 11:00 a.m.- 5:00 p.m.

34. ***American Girl Doll Store*** – 2020 Chesterfield Mall, Chesterfield. (877) 247-5223. This store has everything you need for the very popular American Girl Dolls, including clothes for the doll and matching for the child, books, doll hair salon, dining and birthday parties.

35. ***Swing-A-Round Miniature Golf and Batting Cages*** – 3541 Bogey Rd., St. Charles. (636) 947-4487. Take I-70 west to St. Charles county, get off at the Zumbehl Rd. exit to the south outer road, and it's before Cave Springs Rd. Fun miniature golf with water fountains, and castle and challenging 18 holes! There is also a game room and birthday party room with different party packages available. Miniature golf is $6.50 adults, and $5.50 children, and Mon. - Fri. before 5 pm. it's 75 cents off.

36. ***Whittle Shortline Railroad*** – 24 Front St., Valley Park. (636) 861-3334 (near Highway 141 and Marshall Rd., and Carol House Furniture) This miniature hand-crafted wooden train factory and toy store is located in the Frisco Hotel. Children can play with the largest ever train table in the store and at the same time hear the real trains go by. Train pieces, tracks, and compatible Brio and Thomas pieces can be purchased here. There is open play and different fun activities for children to do. Hours are Tues. – Fri. 10:00 am to 4:00 pm; Sat. 9:00 am to 5:00 pm; Sun 12:00 to 5:00 pm. Birthday parties are also available here.

37. ***Family Golfplex*** – 3717 Tree Court Industrial Blvd. (636) 861-2500. (In Kirkwood, off Marshall Rd.) 18 hole miniature golf with water-falls, fountains, and fun buildings to play through. Fun for the whole family! (There is even a driving range and 9 hole par 3 course for parents and teenagers.) Summer hours are 7:00 am. to 10:00 pm; hours vary for other seasons. $5.00 for adults and $3.50 for children and seniors. Great for Birthday parties!

38. ***Swing-A-Round Fun Town*** – Hwy 141 and Hwy 30 (Gravois); behind the Wal-Mart, Fenton. (636) 349-7077. There are 3 miniature golf courses, bumper boats, batting cages, and go-karts. Miniature golf starts at $5.75. Go-karts are $6.50 for a single seat and $8.00 for a double seat for a 5 to 6 min. ride around the track. Requirements are that you must be at least 54" to drive a go-kart and at least 44" to drive a bumper boat, but younger ones can ride along with an adult.

Mini-go-karts are available to children 3-8 years old. Summer hours are 10 am. to 11 pm. daily. Has Birthday Party packages, too!

39. **The Infield** – 2626 Westhills Park Dr., Ellisville. (You can see it from Manchester Rd., right past Old State Rd.) (636) 458-1144. There is miniature golf ($6.95), batting cages (16 pitches for $1.00) bumper boats ($6.45), go-carts and Jr. go-carts ($7.25). For go-carts you must be 58 inches tall, or 48 inches for jr. go-carts. There is a concession stand for food and drinks, and birthday parties are available. This is a great place for the whole family to have fun. Hours are Mon. – Thurs. 11:00 am to 11:00 pm; Fri. 11:00 am. to 12 midnight; Sat 10:00 am to 12 midnight; Sun. 10:00 am to 11:00 pm.

40. **Grand Prix Karting** – 3500 S. Hwy 94, St. Charles. (Hwy I-70 west to St. Charles to left on Hwy 94, then right on to Jungs Station Rd. and left on service rd.) (636) 946-4848. Ride a go-kart around the track for $10.00! There are two sizes of race tracks with different requirements. Summer hours are 10 am. to 12 midnight seven days a week.

41. **Hardee's Iceplex** – 16851 N. Outer Forty, Chesterfield. (636) 537-4200. Take Highway 40 west to the Chesterfield Airport exit. This ice skating complex has public skating available for $5.00. Skate rental is free. Call for daily schedule of hours.

42. **Dog Museum** – 1721 S. Mason Rd. in Queeny Park. You can only get to it by going in the entrance on Mason Rd., between Manchester Rd. and Clayton Rd. Phone- 821-Dogs. Hours Tues. - Sat., 10:00 am. - 4:00 pm. Sunday, 1:00 pm - 5:00 pm. . Adults $5.00, children 5-14 is $1.00 and seniors 55 yrs. and older $2.50. Fine arts museum with sculptures and pictures of dogs. Videos on breeds, obedience, etc.

43. **Kennelwood Pet Resorts** – 2008 Kratky (off Page and Lindbergh) 429-2100. Families can tour the interworkings of a pet service business such as boarding, grooming, and dog training. Call for reservations.

44. **Three Dog Bakery**– 1134 Town and Country Cossing Dr. (Clayton at Woodsmill Plaza) (636) 527-3364 This is a bakery for your dogs! Have your kids bring their dogs to the bakery and choose from Snickerpoodle cookies, Boxer brownies, bone shaped cookies or a bone shaped birthday cake. Open Mon.– Sat. 10:00 a.m. to 8:00 p.m.; Sun. 11:00 a.m. to 6:00 p.m.

45. **Skyzone** – 17379 Edison Ave. Chesterfield, in Chesterfield Valley shopping center, behind Home Depot. (636) 530-4550. Closed Mondays, open Tues.-Sun. Call for hours. A sports and entertainment facility that has an extremely large, all padded trampoline field where you can jump or play dodge-ball. There is open play time or you can book a party. Children though adults. It is $10.00 an hour person for open jump, plus $2.00 shoe rental. Wear socks.

46. **Little Fishes Swim School** – 8200 Brentwood Industrial Dr., rear entrance, (off of Manchester Rd., just west of Hanley Rd.) (314) 647-7946. This Mommy and Me swim class is in a warm, 90 degree indoor pool. Classes start for 6 month old children and there is also classes for 3 to 5 year olds, teaching beginning swimming skills while building self-confidence and having fun. Birthday parties are available. www.LittleFishesSwimSchool.com

47. **World Aquarium** – inside of the City Museum - 701 N. 15th Street, downtown. (314) 647-6011. $6.00 per person plus your admission to City Museum. This is a unique hands-on exhibit with "touch-pools" where you can pet a small shark, star fish, crabs, turtles and more. There is a large tank with sting-rays, another with sharks and exhibits you can interact with. You will learn a lot!

48. **St. Louis Mills** – 5555 St. Louis Mills Blvd., Hazelwood. (314) 227-5900. Take I-270 North to Hwy 370 West/Missouri Bottom Rd. exit (#22). Keep left at the ramp and proceed 1 mile to St. Louis Mills Blvd. This is a very large shopping mall and entertainment complex. There is Nascar Speedpark, Glow in the dark Mini Golf, ice skating, a skate park, and more. Hours of entertainment!

49. **Build-a-Bear Workshop** – St. Louis Galleria Mall - (314) 725-8282; Westfield West County Mall - (314) 821-1227. You and your child can pick out the kind of bear you would like to build and stuff it, lovingly put in its heart, give it an air-bath and make out its birth certificate. Many kinds of bears and animals to choose from and prices range from around $10.00 on up. Outfits can be bought separately. Birthday parties can be given here. A very special day. Now at the Zoo and Busch Stadium!

50. **Ballwin Commons Recreation Center** – At The Point, on Old Ballwin Rd., Ballwin. (Off of Manchester Rd. about 3 miles west of 141; turn left onto Old Ballwin Rd., between Elco Chevrolet and Petcare) (636) 227-8950. This is a new recreation center that has a fantastic indoor pool with a 2-story spiral slide, a river-like water current that floats

you along a course, a playground in the water for the younger ones with a mini-slide and water-guns, a lap swim area, and a whirlpool. There is also a basketball court, a game room, a work-out area and track for adults, a snack bar, and showers and lockers. Admission ranges from $4.00 to $7.00 depending on age and if you are a resident of Ballwin. Non-resident fees are $7.00 and children 2 years and younger are free. Open swim times vary, call for hours.

51. **Faust Park Carousel –** 15185 Olive - In Faust Park- (636) 537-0222. Highway 40 to Clarkson Rd.(Olive) Turn right and go a few miles. Park is on left. Building houses refurbished Merry-go-round from the old Highlands Park in St. Louis. Hours are Tues. - Sun. 10 am to 4:00 pm. Rides are $1.00 per person. Birthday parties are also available here. Also on the grounds is the restored house of Frederick Bates, the second Governor of Missouri. There is also a historical village. On weekends, noon until 5:00 pm, you can walk among the 19th century buildings and see historical artists performing their crafts. Also visit the Butterfly House.

52. **Butterfly House –** 15193 Olive - in Faust Park, Chesterfield - (636) 530-0076. (See direction above.) This beautiful glass butterfly house has tropical rain forest atmosphere with lots of tropical plants and a waterfall. Over 1,500 butterflies fly freely among you and some may even land right on you! Hours are 9:00am - 5:00pm daily in the summer; and 9:00am - 4:00pm in the winter, except Mondays. Admission is $6.00 adults, $4.50 seniors, $4.00 children 4 to 12 years, and free for children 3 years and under. Free on the 1st Tues. of each month from 9 a.m. to 11 a.m. for St. Louis County and City residents. There are also exhibits, a movie, a gift shop, and group educational rooms are available.

53. **Chesterfield Sports Fusion –** 140 Long Rd. (at Edison Ave.) Chesterfield. (636) 536-6720. This sports complex has Laser Tag ($7.00); a rock climbing wall ($5.00); mini-golf ($6.00); dodge ball ($3.00); an indoor playground ($5.00); and much more. Summer hours are open at 12 noon most days. Winter hours open at 4:00 p.m. during the week and 11:00 a.m. on Saturday, 12:00 p.m. on Sunday. Closed on Tuesdays.

54. **Jamestown Sports Complex –** 5105 N. Highway 67, Florissant. 355-5363. In this sports complex you can sign up for league indoor soccer, indoor softball, karate, roller-hockey, volleyball, summer day camp, summer D.A.R.E. dances, and birthday parties! Lots of fun activities going on the year around. A public pool is open summer evenings 5 p.m to 10 p.m.

West of St. Louis County

55. ***St. Peter's Plex*** – 5200 Mexico Rd., St. Peters. (Take I-70 west to the Cave Springs exit. Turn left and go to 2nd stoplight and turn right onto Mexico Rd. and it's about 2 miles on the left, next to St. Peters City Hall) (636) 939-2386. This is a recreation complex that has indoor ice skating, indoor pool with several separate pools, including kids play area, a gym for basketball, a fitness room, a rock climbing wall, an outdoor in-line skating rink, a family changing room, and a food court. One price is good for the whole day of activities! There are prices for St. Peters residents, St. Charles county residents, and St. Louis metro area residents. St. Louis area resident fee is adults $7.00, children $4.75, and under 12 years $2.50. Call for daily schedule of when each area is open.

56. ***River City Rascals Minor League Professional Baseball*** – T.R. Hughes Ballpark, O'Fallon, MO (about 35 miles west of downtown St. Louis), (636) 240-BATS or toll-free (888) 762-BATS. This is a new ballpark with the old-time ballpark feel. It is good family fun and a relaxing way to spend the summer. You can get season tickets or buy individual tickets in advance online or at the ticket booth the day of the game. Tickets run from $5.00 for lawn sitting (bring your own lawn chairs) up to $11.00 for the best club seats. Game times are Mon.–Sat. 7:05 p.m. and Sundays at 6:05 p.m. Call or visit the website for the schedule at www.rivercityrascals.com. Directions: Take I-70 west (beyond St. Charles and St. Peters, MO) T.R. Hughes Blvd. and turn right and continue until you see the Ballpark and parking.

57. ***Valley Mount Ranch*** – Highway I-44 and Highway 141 Jct. (use Fenton exit; turn left onto 141 and then right) (636) 225-5243. Horseback riding lessons start at $35 for 1 hour with price breaks for additional persons. Appointments needed.

58. ***Six Flags*** – Eureka, Mo. Located about 30 miles southwest of St. Louis on I-44. Take Allenton Exit. (636) 938-5300. Summer hours daily 10:00 am.- 10:00 pm. Fall hours Sat. and Sun. only 10:00 am.- 6:00 pm. Admission is $49.99 per person, or under 48" tall is $36.99, and 3 years and under is free. Buy tickets online and print them out for $39.99 per person for everyone. Parking is $18.00. This is a very large theme park with over 100 rides, shows and adventures and a section for the smaller children too. Now open, the Hurricane Harbor Water Park, which is included in the entrance fee. This has slides, wave pool, a raft ride, and a children's play area. There is a changing area too. Sounds like a great place to be on a hot

St. Louis summer day! Call for information about special coupons, discounts and season passes.

59. **Purina Farms** – Gray Summit, MO. 982-3232. Reservations required but admission free (about a 45 min. drive from Kirkwood). Take I-44 to Gray Summit exit. Go north (right) 2 blocks on Highway 100. Turn left on County Rd. MM and proceed 1 mile to farm entrance. Summer hours are Tues. – Sun. reservations starting at 9:30 a.m. to 3 p.m. Spring and Fall hours are Wed. – Fri. reservations starting at 9:30 a.m. to 1:00 p.m.; Sat. and Sun. reservations starting at 9:30 a.m. to 3 p.m. Demonstration farm with various breeds of cows, horses, sheep, chickens, and pigs. An excellent opportunity to observe baby animals at different growth stages. A clean well-kept farm. Barn with petting areas. Hay loft to play in with rope swing, straw tunnels and an area to ride toy tractors. Dog show, special cat and dog house, milking demos, wagon rides, and gift shop. Snack bar area and inside or outside tables.

60. **Wabash Frisco and Pacific Mini-Steam Railroad** – Glencoe, Mo. (636) 587-3538. 11:00 am. - 4:15pm on Sundays only. May - October Located halfway between Ellisville and Eureka, Mo. The station is half mile down Washington-Grand Ave. from the intersection of old State Road and Hwy 109. Ride a scaled down to size steam train 3 miles roundtrip along the scenic Meramec River. The journey will last about 30 minutes. Admission $4.00 per person, children 3 and under free. Soda machines on property and picnicking available about 1 mile away at Rockwoods Reservation Park.

61. **Daniel Boone Home** – 1868 Highway F., Defiance, Mo. (636) 798-2005. Take Highway 40 west to Highway 94. Turn left onto Highway 94. Go past Busch Wildlife Area to Highway F. This was Daniel Boone's home he built. There are many handmade furnishings and tools. A guide will show you around and tell you many interesting historical facts. Open 9:00 am to 5:00 pm Mon. - Sat.; and Sun. 12:00 to 5:00 pm. You must be there at least 1 1/2 hours before closing to take the tour. There is a restaurant and picnic tables. Adults $7.00, seniors $6.00 and children 4 to 11 are $4.00. A new "frontier village" has been added to the back of the Boone home. There are several shops and a church and school, and the people are dressed in period costumes and work on crafts. If you combine the Village Tour fee with the admissions price, you can get a discounted price for both tours.

62. **Meramec Caverns** – Stanton, Mo. 1 - (573) - 468-3166. Take I-44 West about 60 miles (about 1 hour). Take exit 230 and turn left. There are lots of signs on the highway to direct you. Hours in the summer are 8:30 am. to 7:30 pm. and hours vary in the fall and winter. Adults are $19.00 and children 5-11 years are $9.50. Under 5 years is free but I don't recommend too much under 5 years old. You enter the cave by first going through a gift shop and restaurant, then in the back is the entrance. It is a well guided tour of 1 1/2 miles and they tell you some of the history of the cave. The tour takes 1 hour and 20 minutes, winding along a lighted path. (No strollers allowed.) Spectacular sights. A cave is about 60 degrees year-round so even in August a sweatshirt is recommended. For a whole day's adventure there are picnic tables, canoes, and camping available.

Local Places

63. **Shopping Malls** – Area malls have monthly calendars available with planned activities for children.

- Plaza Frontenac - (314) 432-0604

- Chesterfield Mall - (636) 532-0777

- St. Louis Center - (314) 231-1243

- St. Louis Galleria - (314) 863-5500

- South County Center - (314) 892-5203

- Union Station Plaza - (314) 421-6655

- West county Center - (314) 288-2020

- St. Louis Mills - (314) 227-5900

64. **Union Station Plaza** also has tours of the plaza for groups of children age 3rd grade and up. The 1 hour walking tour, Monday through Friday, includes history of the railroads, history of Union Station, and the redevelopment of the station. Please call for group information about reservations and cost at 421-6655. Paddle boats are available to rent to paddle around a small courtyard lake. $4.00 for 15 minutes. Also in the courtyard is a ferris wheel and merry-go-round. Memories Museum is on the 2nd floor and features model trains, photos, and memorabilia when Union Station was a busy train station. Free and open during regular mall hours.

65. **Local Fire Departments** – take the kids to any fire department and if they have the time they will show you all around the station and let the children sit in the fire trucks. For large groups please make reservations.

66. **Local Library** – Most libraries have story hours, films and events for children. Check with your library for days and times.

67. **The Fine Arts** – There are several wonderful organizations that can help expose your children to the fine arts.

(a) **Young Audiences Inc.** – 968-5554. Monday through Friday 8:30 am. to 4:30 pm. This touring group will perform at schools and other organizations. They give plays which incorporate music, and musical performances to suit any age level. I have seen "Little Red Riding Hood", "Folk Trio" (a collection of American folk songs), and "Pilgrim Courage", all which are excellent for preschoolers on up. "The 60s, The Times They are a Changing" is an insight for high schoolers, and an emotional remembrance for those of us who lived through it. This group is highly recommended. You may call for a monthly schedule of performances. Some are open to the general public. Children and adults will enjoy themselves.

(b) **Metro Theater Company** – 997-6777. Monday through Friday 9:00 am. to 5:00 pm. This is a touring company that mixes music with a play. They have several plays a year that they perform for schools and other organizations. Coming up is "Go Dog Go," and "Moby" (the story from the Whale's prespective), and many more. Call for a schedule of events.

(c) **Fontbonne Theater for Children** – 6800 Wydown Blvd., Clayton. 889-1425. They have a children's play yearly, usually in the spring. The play runs for about 2 weeks. Call for dates and times.

(d) **Florissant Civic Center Theatre** – 1 Civic Center Dr., Florissant. 921-5678. They have 4 to 5 plays for children during the school year, all performed by different traveling companies. Call for names of plays, dates, and times.

(e) **Kinder Konzert Series** – Powell Symphony Hall, 718 North Grand Blvd., St. Louis. 533-2500. Concerts for kids! The St. Louis Symphony has a concert series especially designed for children which includes mimes and dance companies. Call for dates and times.

(f) **Craft Alliance** – 6640 Delmar, St. Louis. 725-1177. An art gallery and classes for children and adults, in pottery, drawing, painting, sculpturing, fabric design, and others. Children as young as 3 years are accepted for classes. Call for hours.

(g) **COCA for Kids** – The Center of Contemporary Arts – 524 Trinity Ave., University City, 725-6555. Classes in dance, music, theatre and storytelling for the preschoolers on up.

(h) **Piwacket Theater** – A children's theater that travels to different places around the city. Call for performances. 963-8800.

68. **BOOK STORES** – There are many, many good book stores in our area, but this is a list of bookstores that I have visited that have a large selection of children's books.

(a) **Barnes & Noble** – West County Mall, Des Peres. 835-9980; 8871 Ladue Rd., Ladue, 862-6280; 9618 Watson Rd., Crestwood, 843-9480. They have a separate room for children's books and have story hours and special presentations. Call for a schedule.

(b) **Pudd'nhead Books** – 8157 Big Bend, Old Orchard Webster, (314) 918-1069.

(c) **Green Trails Bookshop** – 14270 Ladue Rd., Chesterfield. 576-7758. Large children's selection.

(d) **Webster Groves Bookshop** – 100 W. Lockwood, Webster. 968-1185. Large selection of children's books.

(e) **Main Street Books** – 307 S. Main St., St. Charles. (636) 949-0105. Very cute book store with large selection of children's books.

My Additions to
Museums and Entertainment

My Additions to
Museums and Entertainment

PARKS

PARKS

There are many, many wonderful parks in the St. Louis area (and some that are OK but not worth going a second time). I am listing some of my favorite parks, but I know there are plenty that I have not yet discovered. Most of these parks are listed with the South County Parks and Recreation Dept. For information call 615-7275 Monday - Friday 8:00 am.- 4:30 pm.

1. *Babler Memorial State Park* – Highway 109- take Manchester Rd. west past Ballwin, past Ellisville, till Highway 109, turn right and follow highway to park. Park- (636) 458-3813. Very large state park, 2,400 acres, with camping, hiking trails, picnicking, swimming pool, and playgrounds.

2. *Bee-Tree Park* – Becker and Finestown Rd. Take I-270 South to Telegraph Rd. Turn right and go about 5 miles to Becker Rd. Turn left and go about 2 miles. The park is on the corner of Becker and Finestown Rd. 615-7275. Park overlooks the Mississippi River. Beautiful and peaceful grounds with lakes, trails, playground, and picnic areas.

3. *Busch Memorial Wildlife Area* – Weldon Springs, Mo., St. Charles County. (636) 441-4554. Take Highway 40 west to Highway 94. Turn left on 94 and go about 1 mile and turn right on Route D. Entrance is a few miles down on the right. This would be a great place for a Father-Son type day. There is a marked auto tour you can drive and see many facets of nature. There are also hiking paths, fishing, and hunting in the proper seasons and with permits.

4. *Des Peres Park* – on the corner of Manchester Rd. and Ballas Rd. 966-4252. Playground in front of park and lake for fishing and ducks in the back. No fishing permit is needed for children 15 and under. Picnic tables around the lake and playground.

5. *Faust Park* – 15185 Olive. Take Highway 40 west to Clarkson/Olive exit. Turn right and go a few miles and the park is on the left. There is an indoor merry-go-round ((636) 537-0222) refurbished from the old Highlands Park in St. Louis. Hours are Tues. through Sun. 10:00 am to 4:00 pm. Rides are $2.00 per person. In the park is also a playground, picnic tables, and a restored house that belonged to Frederick Bates, the second Governor of Missouri. On weekends, noon until 5 p.m., you can walk among the 19th century buildings of Faust Historical Village and watch the blacksmith and other historical

artists perform their crafts. Free. A Butterfly House ((636) 530-0076) is on the grounds. This is a glass conservatory filed with tropical plants and over 1,500 butterflies that fly freely among the visitors. Hours are 9:00 a.m. to 5:00 p.m. daily, in the summer. Winter hours are 9:00 am - 4:00 pm, except Mondays. Admission is $6.00 for adults, $4.50 for seniors, $4.00 for children under 12 years, and free for children 3 and under. Free on the 1st Tuesday of the month from 9:00 a.m. to 11:00 a.m.

6. ***Forest Park*** – Highway 40 and Hampton Ave. In Forest Park is the Zoo, Science Center, Art Museum, and Jefferson Memorial. See separate listings under Museums and Entertainment section.

7. ***Greensfelder Park*** – Allenton Rd. - take I-44 West to Six Flags exit, Allenton Rd. Turn right and road will lead to park. 615-7275. Very large park, 1,700 acres. Hiking, picnicking, playgrounds, and hay-rides. Horses – Brookdale Farms (636) 615-4386.

8. ***Kirkwood Park*** – Geyer and Adams Rd. From Kirkwood Rd. take Adams Rd. west and it will take you to park. 822-5855. Lots of shady picnic tables, playground, snack stand in the summer, sprinkler in the summer, ballfields, and tennis courts. There is year-round ice skating at the recreation complex on Geyer Rd. Call park for skating hours. There is a big, new fishing lake. There is a water park for Kirkwood residents and their guests.

9. ***Katy Trail*** – Missouri River State Trail – This is a newly developed hiking and bicycle trail. It is Missouri's longest and skinniest park – 255 miles long and 100 feet wide! Sections of the trail were open but check with MO State Parks (1-800-334-6946) because some sections of the trail close because of periodic flooding. (take I-70 to right on 5th St., then right on Boonslick Rd. to riverfront and the Katy Trail entrance), to Weldon Springs Wildlife Area in St. Charles County (Highway 94 and 40) to Defiance, to Augusta, to Marthasville. The crushed limestone, flat path makes the trail accessible to bikers, hikers, wheelchairs, families with small children, and seniors. For the Weldon Springs entrance, take Highway 40 west to Highway 94. Turn left onto 94 and go 5.3 miles and you will see a sign that says River Access and another that says Hiking and Biking Trail. Turn left on gravel road and you'll come to a parking lot. Park and there will be an entrance to the Katy Trail. At this point you can either ride your bike back 5 miles to the Highway 40/Missouri River bridge or go ahead 9 miles to Augusta or 12 more miles after Augusta to Marthasville. There are places to stop for refreshments in Augusta

and Defiance and even a bicycle rental shop. There is another parking lot and entrance in Augusta. The trail is open only during daylight hours. Helmets are advised.

10. **Laumeier Sculpture Park** – 12580 Rott Rd. Take Lindbergh Rd. south past Watson Rd. and turn west onto Rott Rd. (stop light at the corner). Large outdoor sculptures on the beautiful and peaceful grounds. You can picnic on the grass or follow the paved paths that wander through the grounds, or let the kids run and skip on acres of grass. (Paths are great for little ones still in strollers, mine have taken naps as we strolled along!) Also Art Gallery and Arts Education Buildings. Gallery hours Tues. - Sat. 10:00 am. - 5:00 pm., Sun. 12:00 pm. - 5:00 pm. Park hours 8:00 am. to half hour after sunset. There are children's art classes offered in drawing, painting, clay, cartooning and more. Ages 7 through adult.

11. **Lone Elk Park** – I-44 West to Hwy 141 -turn right at the bottom of the ramp then right again onto North Outer Rd. Turn left at stop sign onto North Outer Rd., which will dead end into the park. 615-7275. Wildlife refuge area with bison, elk, deer, ducks, wild turkeys, etc. You mainly stay in your car and ride through the park seeing the animals in the woods, water, and on the side of the road. You'll see more animals in the early morning and evening. There are picnic areas. Park closes half hour after sunset. Free.

12. **World Bird Sanctuary** – A new Environmental Educational Center is just outside the entrance gates of Lone Elk Park. You can learn about birds of prey and see eagles, hawks, owls and many more birds up close. Open 7 days a week from 8:00 am - 5:00 pm. Visitors information center open from 11:00 am - 3:00 pm. (636) 225-4390. Special programs are shown several times a year.

13. **Wild Canid Survival and Research Center/Wolf Santuary** – (636) 938-5900 At Washington University's Tyson Research Center in Eureka. Take I-44 West to Beaumont/Antire Rd. exit; turn right. Tours of the center are by reservation only. Hours and prices vary according to the programs. There are several kinds of programs including Sat. tours, campfire programs, and wolf programs. www. wolfsanctuary.org. Call or check website, as they may be relocating soon.

14. **John Allan Love Park** – Mason Lane, off Manchester Rd. Take Manchester Rd. west past I-270, past the city of Des Peres, and turn left onto Mason Lane, which is 1 block past the White Castle. 615-

7275. Beautiful park with lots of trees and hiking trails, and 2 play-grounds in wooded areas. There are several sheltered picnic areas, fire pits, and ballfields.

15. **Mastodon State Park** – Take I-55 south of Highway 141. Take the Kimmswick/Imperial exit then turn right and go a block. There is first a picnic entrance and a block further is the museum entrance. Near Kimmswick, Mo. (636) 464-2976. There is a museum ($2.50 for adults and children 14 years and under free) with a skeleton of a mastodon, and several tusks and bones on display which are over 10,000 years old. Archeologists have found these bones, and man-made instruments on excavation sites in the park. A 10 min. slide show will show you the history of the Mastodons. The park is open from 9:00 am. to 4:30 pm. Monday through Saturday, and from noon to 4:30 pm. on Sunday. There are picnicing facilities and hiking trails.

16. **North County Recreation Complex** – Redman Rd. 355-7373. Take I-270 North to Highway 367 North to Redman Rd. There are several playgrounds and tennis courts.

17. **Queeny Park** – 550 Weidman Rd., Ballwin. Take Manchester Rd. west into Ballwin, turn right on Weidman Rd. (Stop light there and Kentucky Fried Chicken on opposite corner.) Go about 1 mile - entrance on the right. There is also another entrance to the park, primarily for the Dog Museum and hiking trails, from Mason Rd. between Manchester Rd. and Clayton Rd. Park- (636) 391-0900. Dog Museum- 821-DOGS (see Museum and Entertainment) . Large playground with lots of equipment, picnic areas, hiking trails, and lake.

18. **Rockwoods Reservation** – Glencoe Rd, Pond, Mo. I-44 west to Eureka exit, and north on Highway 109. Or Manchester Rd. (Highway 100) west past Ellisville and left onto Highway 109. (636) 458-2236. Very large conservation area and an educational center on wildlife resources and forestry, hiking trails, and picnic areas.

19. **South County Recreation Complex** – 6050 Wells Rd. Take I-270 south to Highway 21 (Tesson Ferry Rd.) Turn right or west, and go about 3 miles (pass McDonald's) then turn left on Wells Rd. and go about 1 mile, entrance on the left. 894-3088. Nice playground area with lots of climb-on objects. Public swimming pool and tennis courts. Picnicking across the street at Suson Park.

20. **Suson Park** – 6050 Wells Rd. Take I-270 south to Highway 21 (Tesson Ferry Rd.) Turn right or west, and go about 3 miles (pass McDonald's) then turn left on Wells Rd. and go about I mile, entrance on the right. (South County Complex on the left) 615-7275. Suson Park has a great farm for the kids to walk around. Horses, pigs, goats, chickens, cows, bulls etc. Free. The park also has a large stocked fishing lake with a bait shop and snack bar. No fishing permit needed for children 15 and under. Several playgrounds and lots of picnic areas. Winter hours for the farm are October 15 through March; Saturday, and Sunday from 10:00 am. to 3:30 pm. Summer hours Mon. - Fri. 10:30 am - 5:00 pm, and Sat. and Sun. 10:30 am - 7:00 pm.

21. **Tilles Park** – McKnight Rd. and Litzsinger Rd. Take Manchester Rd. east to McKnight Rd., turn left and go about I mile to Litzsinger Rd. 615-7275. A wonderful playground in the front of the park and many picnic areas in groves of shade trees. Fishing lake (no permit needed for children 15 and under). This is the park that also has a beautiful Christmas light display in Dec.

22. **Turtle Park** – Oakland Ave. and Tamm. (On Oakland Ave. just east of Skinker and south of Forest Park. You can see it from Highway 40) This is a little park with great big turtles to climb on! Sculptor Robert Cassilly made an area of enchantment out of concrete, by creating 3 large turtles, 4 smaller ones, turtle eggs hatching and a snake, all for the delight of children to play on. The snake even turns into a bench to rest upon.

23. **Watson Trails Park** – 12450 W. Watson, in Sunset Hills- Take Lindbergh south and turn right at Eddie and Park Rd. (West Watson Rd. when turning right) 1 block on the left side. Nice smaller park. Has great playground for the smaller children. There is a fishing lake you can walk around and feed the ducks (fishing permit $1.00 for children). Hiking trails are mulch lined and good even for the little ones and every trail leads back to lake or playground. Also swimming pool and tennis courts for residents or guests of residents of Sunset Hills.

24. **Orienteering Club** – 7206 Lindell, St. Louis, MO 63130. Sloc. us.orienteering.org. A sport for the whole family in which you follow a preset course with the help of a detailed map and check points. Planned events are held at different parks in the county and state. For the young children there is a course that you follow a string through the woods, for the nature lovers you can take your time and

enjoy the woods, and for the competitors, you can race time and finish the course at your best speed.

25. **St. Louis County Parks and Recreation Department** sponsors a Nature Program series at various parks throughout the year. For registration and more information call 615-7275.

26. **Castlewood State Park** – Park office - (636) 527-6481. Take Manchester Rd. west into Ballwin, and turn left on New Ballwin Rd. at the stop light. Go a few miles, stay straight when the road forks to left at Big Bend. Follow Castlewood Park signs to Kiefer Creek Rd. and Castlewood Rd. You will see park entrance. Wonderful big park along the Meramec River; very scenic and many bicycle and hiking trails. There are picnic areas and a boat launch.

27. **Powder Valley Conservation Nature Center** – 11715 Cragwold Rd., Kirkwood. 301-1500. Take Geyer Rd. south past Big Bend, and turn right on Cragwold Rd. (right before you get to the overpass of I-44). Go a mile or so and there is a large stone entrance way. The nature center consists of 112 acres, several hiking trails, an outdoor staging area, and a beautiful new building housing the Missouri Department of Conservation and a hands-on nature center focusing on wildlife in an urban setting. Some of the exhibits include a Tree House that children can walk inside, animal masks they can put on, a theater that kids can put on their own puppet show, and an underwater viewing pond full of fish! Hours are 8:00 am. to 5:00 p.m. everyday.

28. **Route 66 State Park** – 97 North Outer Rd (of I-44), Eureka. (636) 938-7198. I-44 West to Lewis Rd. exit. This park is part of the famous Old Route 66 Highway. There are 7 miles of paths open for hiking, bicycling, and horseback riding. Some of the paths go by the peaceful Meramec River. It is all flat, so it is easy for even small children who are just learning to ride a bike. There is a visitors center which is full of Route 66 memorabilia. Visitors center is open 9:00 am. to 5:00 pm daily.

29. **Trailnet** – 3900 Reavis Barracks Rd. 416-9930. There are many hiking and biking trails that have opened recently. Most were opened by Trailnet and now are run by the St. Louis County parks. There is Grants trail, in South County, near I-55, Union Rd. and Hoffmeister, behind the Orlando Garden that goes all they way to Crestwood and Kirkwood, and there is the Old Chain of Rocks Bridge Trail, and there is a West Alton, MO trail, also a Riverfront trail, downtown, and many

more trails to come. Call Trailnet for directions or email at trailnet@
trailnet.org.

30. ***Shaw Arboretum or Shaw Nature Reserve*** – Gray Summit, MO (636)
451-3512. Take I-44 west (about 22 miles from the junction of I-44
and I-270) to the Gray Summit exit which is Highway 100. Turn left
onto crossing the bridge, turn right, and the entrance will be on the
left. This park, which is owned by the Missouri Botanical Garden, has
about 12 miles of beautiful hiking trails through various natural envi-
ronments. You first enter the Visitors Center and get a map of 7 different trails you can hike, including a wildflower trail, a prairie grass
trail, and a river trail. Length of the trails vary from a short stroll, a
1 or 2 mile hike, to joining the trails together for an all day outing.
Admission is $5.00 for adults, $3.00 for seniors and children 12 and
under are free. Members of Missouri Botanical Gardens are free.
Park hours are 7:00 a.m. to 1/2 hour past sunset daily, Visitor Center
hours are 8:00 a.m. to 4:30 p.m. daily. Closed during deer season.

31. ***Elephant Rocks State Park*** – About a 2 hour drive south on Highway
21. This is a fun day trip for the whole family. Pack a picnic and
sodas and enjoy a day outside. The park gets its name from the bil-
lion year old granite boulders that are as big as, and even bigger than
elephants! Children can run and climb and slide down the smooth,
rounded boulders. There is also a paved path that lets you wander
around the boulders. Picnic tables and outhouses are available.

32. ***Johnson's Shut-Ins State Park*** – About a 2 hour drive south on
Highway 21, pass Elephant Rocks State Park and take the next right
onto Highway N and go 12 miles. This is a very large State Park with
picnic and camping facilities. The feature most loved about this park
is the Black River flowing through the middle of the boulders forming
waterfalls, slides, and pools for people to play in. If you have very
young children, you might want to stay at the edge of the river. To
play in the river you have to be able to jump from boulder to boulder.
Very refreshing on a hot day! The view is spectacular; Mother Nature
at her best. Bring a picnic, old tennis shoes for the water, and a
swim suit or change of clothes.

33. ***Ulysses S. Grant National Historic Site*** – 7400 Grant Rd. (next to the
parking lot of Grant's Farm) (314) 842-3298. Open daily 9:00 am -
5:00 pm. Free admission. There are several historic structures in this
National Park, including the house from the family of Julia Dent, the
wife of Civil War General and 18th US President Grant. The Visitor

Center has many interesting exhibits and a short movie. Junior Ranger activities are available to children.

34. *Longview Farm Park* – 13525 Clayton Rd., Town and Country. There is an old farm house with a horse barn and pastures. There is over 30 acres of beautiful wooded areas with paved or mulch paths that wander through streams, ponds, bridges and decks. Catch and release fishing is allowed. There are at least 27 different species of Missouri trees identified and labeled for your convenience. There is also a wonderful playground area with restrooms available. This is a very peaceful and relaxing park.

My Additions
to Parks

Seasonal Events

ECKERTS

SEASONAL EVENTS

For information on special events you can call The St. Louis Convention and Visitors Commission at 421-1023.

Christmas Time

1. ***Tilles Park*** – Litzsinger and McKnight Rds., Ladue. 615-7275. In December in the evenings is a beautiful Christmas light display, with a river of lights, waterfalls, Santa's sleigh and many others all lit up. You drive all through the park and see miles of lights. Hours are 5:30 p.m. to 9:30 p.m. the day after Thanksgiving until after New Years Day. Closed every Saturday, Dec. 24 and Dec. 31. Tickets are $9.00 per car load and are bought at the gate.

2. ***Lady of the Snows*** – 9500 West Illinois Rt. 15, Belleville, Ill. 314-241-3400. Another beautiful light display with a religious theme. Take Highway 40 east and cross over the Mississippi River at Poplar St. Bridge. You are on I-64 (Highway 40) about 4 miles, then go east on I-255 about 3 miles, then south to Route #15, then about 1 1/2 miles further you'll see the entrance. Starts the day after Thanksgiving, 5-10 pm. Donations are taken.

3. ***Santa's Magical Kingdom*** – Eureka, MO. (636) 938-5925. Take I-44 west to the Six Flags exit, turn left and follow signs. Wonderful Christmas light display, 35 acres of sparkling lights, animated figures, and joyful Christmas Music. See Yogi Bear, the Flintstones, a candycane village, and Santa's workshop. Open mid-November to early January 5:30 pm. to 10:30 pm. daily. A carload for around $19.00. Well worth it!

4. ***Breakfast with Santa*** – Macy's Downtown has a program in December where kids can have a breakfast with Santa and many elves. There is singing, magic, clowns and balloons. Great time for all. Call the store for dates and times. An ad is usually in the paper in early November to give dates. Call early because it fills fast.

5. ***Anheuser–Busch Holiday Light Display*** – At Anheuser-Busch Brewery, Pestalozzi and Arsenal St The buildings and trees are all outlined in beautiful lights for their annal display. you can drive by 6 pm until midnight. Free.

6. ***Magic House*** – 516 S. Kirkwood Rd., Kirkwood. 822-8900. In the middle of December, kids can come and make Christmas crafts and there is a special Chrismas program. Please call for days and hours.

7. *Santa Comes to Museum of Transport* – 3015 Barrett Station Rd. 965-7998. Santa visits children at the Museum in late November. Call for day and time. Treats, refreshments, and tours of the museum will also be available. In mid-December there is a Teddy Bear Tea in the Creation Station.

8. *Santa Comes to the Dogs!* – Kennelwood Pet Resorts - 2008 Kratky (Off Page and Lindbergh) 429-2100. Also available at Kennelwood's Pet Depots at #4 Clarkson Centre, Chesterfield, (636) 537-3221; South County, #40 Ronnie's Plaza, 849-8118; St. Peters, 418 S. Church St., (636) 970-4411; and 2216 Mason Lane, Ballwin, 822-3500. Annual photo event for the whole family, including the family pet. Pictures of your pet may be taken with Santa, the family, or alone. A variety of package prices are available with a portion going to charity. You can also make Christmas cards or Christmas ornaments from the photos. Great family fun; many families return year after year for their annual portrait. Starts November until the week before Christmas. Call for days, times, and reservations.

9. *Christmas on Eckert's Farm* – Eckert's Farm, 901 S. Green Mount Rd., Belleville IL, (618) 233-0513. Enjoy a special family Christmas breakfast, photo with Santa, face painting, clown, and more. End the breakfast with a wagon ride with Santa. Call early for date, time, and fee. Also, in early December, children and families can come assemble their own gingerbread house. Everything is provided. Houses can be assembled in 45 mins. and each one is a creative masterpiece! Call for date, times, and fee.

10. *Oakland House* – 7801 Genesta Rd, off Heege Rd, Affton. 352-5654. Annual Christmas House for children with puppet show, storyteller and a visit with Santa and a cookie baked by Mrs. Claus. Call for day, times, and cost.

11. *Nutcracker Suite Ballet* – Performed by St. Louis Ballet at Edison Theatre - Washington University. (314) 935-6543. Call for times and prices.

12. *Eugene Field House* – 634 S. Broadway, downtown. 421-4689. A museum decorated for Christmas as it was in the 1800s. An old-fashioned Christmas tree and decorations. Adults $5.00, children 4-11 years is $1.00, under 3 years old is Free.

13. *Missouri Botanical Gardens* – 4344 Shaw - 577-5100- In Dec. they have their annual holiday display. Each year is a different theme.

Open 9:00 am. to 5:00 pm. daily. Holiday Display is $3.00 in addition to regular admission. Regular admission, adults $4.00 for St. Louis City and County residents, and $8.00 for adults who are not St. Louis City or County residents and children free. Wed. and Sat. from 9:00 am. to noon is free for St. Louis City and County residents.

14. *Skate with Santa* – Steinberg Ice Rink, Forest Park. (314) 367-7465. Open during the Christmas Season, please call for days, times and prices to ice skate with Santa.

15. *Festival of Trees* – Location varies each year, call 849-4440. The display starts a few weeks before Thanksgiving. There is a small admissions fee. There are over 100 decorated Christmas trees, a talking tree, trains, craft booths, a store where children can buy gifts, and a booth where children can create their own ornaments; and of course Santa! Snacks available.

16. *Christmas Traditions* – St. Charles Historic District on Main St. Sat. and Sundays in December at 1:30 pm. is a Santa Parade with Santa's from around the world and through history. Christmas Carolers and family activities are along Main St. See website www.stcharleschristmas.com

17. *Annual Downtown Christmas Parade* – The parade with floats, marching bands and Santa is Thanksgiving Day morning from 9:00 am. to 11:00 am. Check the paper for the route.

18. *Ice Skate with Santa* – Holiday Ice Skating at Kennedy Recreation Center at South County Rec.-6050 Wells Dr. . (314) 894-3088. Families can skate with Santa and Listen to holiday music on Sunday in mid Dec. Call for date.

19. *Wild Lights* – St. Louis Zoo. 781-0900. A cute animated light display as you walk through the zoo. $5.00 a person. 5:30 p.m. to 8:30 p.m. Call to see when display starts for the season.

20. *Visit Santa at most of the area shopping centers.* Call your local mall for days and hours.

21. *Cut your own Christmas tree* – There are many places where you can pick your own special tree for Christmas and cut it yourself or have them help. This is a great way for the whole family to get into the Christmas spirit.

(a) **Meert Tree Farms** – Festus and Mehlville locations. The Festus farm is the largest of the two with over 5,000 trees. The Mehlville farm has about 350 trees. Both have Scotch Pines and Douglas Firs, and both are open 9:00 am. to 5:00 pm. starting the day after Thanksgiving through December 23. Hot chocolate and cider will be sold on weekends at the Festus Farm. To get to the Mehlville Farm, take I-270 south and exit on Telegraph Rd. Go south 1 mile to Yaeger Rd. and turn right and go about 1/4 mile. To get to the Festus Farm, take I-55 south to Festus. Drive 3 miles past Highway 67 and turn right at Exit 170 onto Highway 61. Go 1/2 mile and turn left at Jefferson School Rd. and then left again at Highway TT. Go 3 miles to Highway T and turn right and go 3 more miles to the farm. 487-5824.

(b) **Christmas Tree Valley** – Pacific, Mo. (636) 742-3436 and (636) 275-9917. Take I-44 to the second Pacific exit, go south on Highway N, and cross the old Bend Bridge and go 2 miles to the farm. 742-3436. Over 40 acres of Scotch Pines, White Pines and Eastern Red Cedars. They also have some Scotch and White Pines, Norway Spruces and Douglas Firs that are balled and wrapped in burlap. There is a Christmas Village with live animals, and on weekends, a puppet show, a fort, and Santa. Also on weekends they will be selling sandwiches, hot chocolate, and hot cider. Open the day after Thanksgiving until the weekend before Christmas, 9:00 am. to 4:00 pm.

(c) **Pea Ridge Farm** – Near Hermann, Mo. Take I-70 west to the Truxton exit (about 4 miles west of Warrenton) and go south on Highway B for 12 miles to Highway 94. Turn left and go 1 mile to the farm. 932-4687. They have over 3,000 trees, and a haywagon will take you all around. Hot chocolate and coffee are free and hot dogs and soft drinks are for sale in a heated barn area. Open 9:00 am. to 5:00 pm. starting the day after Thanksgiving.

(d) **Eckert's Orchard** – Three Locations –

- Millstadt, Il. Take Poplar St. Bridge to Highway 3 (the 1st Il. exit) and go south. Follow Highway 3 to Highway 157 and go north. Continue to Highway 163. Drive south about 4 miles to the farm. Follow the signs. 618-233-0513.

- Belleville, IL (take Hwy. 40 east (I-64) across the Mississippi River at the Poplar Street Bridge. Stay on I-64 about 4 miles, then go east on

I-255 about 3 miles, then south on Rt. 15, past Rt. 159.) (618) 233-0513.

- Grafton, IL (From Alton take Great River Rd. to Grafton. Turn right on Rt. 3 and left on Otterville Rd. Watch for signs.) (618) 786-3445.

  Scotch and White Pines and Douglas firs are available among these 50,000 trees. Hot cider and hot chocolate available and there is a bonfire, wagon rides, plus Santa on the weekends. Open daily starting the day after Thanksgiving.

22. *Ice Skating Rinks-*

- Affton Ice Rink – 10300 Gravois. 849-0605.

- Brentwood Ice Rink – 2505 Brentwood Blvd. 963-8689. Indoor rink.

- Hardee's Ice Plex – 16851 N. Outer Forty. (636) 537-4200. Indoor Rink

- Creve Coeur Rink - 11400 Old Cabin Rd. 432-3950. Inside rink.

- Forum Ice Rink – Fenton. (636) 349-7860. Indoor Rink.

- Kirkwood Ice Rink – 111 S. Geyer. 822-5825. Indoor rink.

- Queeny Park – 550 Weidman Rd. (636) 391-0900. Inside Rink.

- St. Peters Rec Plex – 5200 Mexico Rd. (636) 939-2386. Indoor rink.

- South County Recreation Complex – 6050 Wells Rd. 894-3088. Indoor rink.

- Steinberg Skating Rink – Forest Park. 367-7465. Outside rink.

- Webster Groves Ice Rink – 33 E. Glendale Rd. 963-5678.

23. *Sled riding at Queeny Park* – Enjoy the beautiful scenery as you and the family slide down the slopes behind Greensfelder Recreation Complex. Open during regular park hours when there is snow on the ground.

Easter Time

1. **Easter Egg Hunts** – At many different local parks. Hazelwood and Berkeley Parks and Recreation both sponsor annual hunts. Queeny Park has just started an annual Easter Egg Hunt and Purina Farms has an Easter Village! Check paper for other listings.

2. **Des Peres Park** usually has an Easter Bunny House. Manchester Rd. and Ballas Rd. Call for day and hours. 966-4252.

3. **Zoo** – Forest Park-781-0900- Have Breakfast with the Bunny! Breakfast will be served and there are many costumed characters to see. There are treats and family photos with the Bunny. Call for reservations, times and cost.

4. **The Magic House** – 516 S. Kirkwood Rd., Kirkwood. 822-8900. Children age II and under will decorate eggs with materials provided. Admission is $8.75.

5. **Eckert's Easter Egg-citement** – Events include an Easter egg hunt, photo with the Easter Bunny, games, plus live chicks and rabbits. Advance reservations required. Belleville Farm only. (618) 233-0513. (see previous page for directions)

Summer Time

1. **Circus Flora** – Look in the newspaper for current location and dates. A wonderful one-ring circus; highly recommended! They perform annually around mid-April till mid-June. High wire acts, clowns, and much more. All performances are interpreted for the hearing impaired. www.circusflora.org

2. **Fair St. Louis (V. P. Fair)** – On the grounds under the Arch. An annual summer event. An annual summer event 4th of July weekend. Lots of top name entertainment, many booths of food and drink, and a spectacular fireworks display nightly.

3. **Festival of Nations** – This gathering is held annually the weekend before Labor Day weekend, at Tower Grove Park; the South-side of St. Louis, at Grand Ave. and Arsenal St. It is celebrating the music, food, crafts and traditions of many countries all over the world. Kids and adults will love it. www.iistl.org

4. **Aquaport** – At Maryland Heights Centre, 2344 McKelvey Rd. 434-1919. This is a great place to be on those hot St. Louis days! It is

a new water park with several kinds of pools to play in. There are 5 different slides, a lazy river to float on a tube in, a lap swim area, a fountain area, and a children's pool area. There are changing rooms and a snack bar area. Hours are 11 am to 7 pm daily. For non-residents of Maryland Heights, adults are $15.00 and children 4-15 years are $10.00. 3 years and under are free.

5. **The Lodge at Des Peres** – 1050 Des Peres Rd., Des Peres. (314) 835-6150. Large aqua center with slides and fun equipment for the kids Outdoor and indoor pool. There are residential and non-residential fees. Call for hours.

6. **South County Recreation Complex** – 6050 Wells Rd. 894-3088. Large pool and kiddie pool; snack bar. Pool open Memorial Day to Labor Day. Hours are Monday and Wednesday 12:00 pm. - 8:00 pm.; Tuesday and Thursday 12:00 pm. - 5:00 pm., with lap swim 5:00 pm. - 6:00 pm.; Friday, Saturday, and Sunday 12:00 pm. - 6:00 pm. Adults-13 $4.00, children 5-12 $3.00, and children under 4 are free.

There are many other city pools but you must be a resident of that city or with a resident to be admitted.

7. **Raging Rivers Waterpark** – Grafton, Illinois. (618) 786-2345. See under Museums and Entertainment.

8. **Blanchette Aquatic Center** – 1900 W. Randolph, St. Charles. 1-(636) 723-4170. Take I-70 to Highway 94 in St. Charles, turn right, then left on Kingshighway, past Lindenwood College. Go until street dead ends at Randolph, on the left a few more blocks. A great swimming park that was redone with all new play equipment in the pool; kind of like a McDonald's playground in a pool! Hours are 11 am. - 7 pm daily, Memorial Day through Labor Day. 12 - Adults are $6.00, 11 - 3 yrs. $5.00 and 2 and under $2.00 for cost of swimming diaper.

9. **McNair Aquatic Center** – 3200 Droste, St. Charles. 1-(636) 724-7001. Same type of playground/pool as Blanchette. Same hours and price.

10. **North Pointe Family Aquatic Center** – 335 Holloway Rd., Ballwin. Call (636) 227-2981. A swim center with a lazy river, a shallow leisure pool, a play pool, lanes for swimming, a toddler area, a waterfall, and a tree with a rope swing! Open to residents and non-residents. For nonresidents the fees are $6.00 for youths 3–18 years and $7.00 for adults.

11. **Great Ice Cream**

(a) Custard Station – W. Argonne Dr., Kirkwood, off of Kirkwood Rd., next to the train station. Popular place to go and eat your cone outside as you watch the trains go by.

(b) Ted Drewes Frozen Custard – 6726 Chippewa- 481-2652, or 4224 S. Grand- 352-7376. This has been a crowd-pleaser for years!

(c) Cold Stone Creamery - many locations. The location at 16 Boulevard St. Louis (near the Galleria; across from Crate & Barrel) gives tours to groups with reservations. (314) 862-6363. Great ice cream!

12. **Peach and Strawberry Picking** – Strawberries are in season from mid-May to mid-June, and peaches are in season from mid-July to August. There are several Eckert's Orchards to choose from. See directions below. The kids delight in finding the fruit for themselves. I can still hear the excitement in their voices as they say, "I see one, I see one!"

Fall and Halloween

1. **Apple picking** – Early September through October- There are many orchards in Missouri and Illinois. You can pick your own apples; the kids love it. They also sell cider and candy apples and some places give wagon rides.

(a) **Eckert's Orchards** – Rt 1 Grafton, Il. From Alton take Great River Rd. to Grafton. Turn right on Rt. 3 and left on Otterville Rd. Watch for signs. 618-786-3445.

(b) **Eckert's Orchards** – Millstadt, Il. From St. Louis take I-255 crossing Jefferson Barracks Bridge. Take Rt. 3 to Highway 158 to Millstadt. Follow signs. 618-233-0513.

(c) **Eckert's Orchards** – Rt. 15, Belleville, IL - Take Highway 40 east (I-64) across the Mississippi River at the Poplar St. Bridge. Stay on I-64 about 4 miles, then go east on I-255 about 3 miles, then south on Rt. 15, past Rt. 159. (618) 233-0513.

(d) **Uncle Andy's Orchard** – Grafton, Il. 618-786-3305.

(e) **Yates Orchards** – Grafton, Il. On Highway 1. 618-498-3752.

(f) **Mills Apple Farm** – R. 1, Marine, IL. Located 3 1/2 miles N.E. of Marine between Marine and Granfork. (618) 887-4732.

2. *Scenic drives to see fall leaves* – There are many places to just drive
    to see all the beautiful leaves changing colors, including Rockwoods
    Reservation, Greensfelder Park, Babler Park, and Lone Elk Park,
    but my very favorite is the ride to and around **Pere Marquette
    State Park, IL.** It's a fun and relaxing days adventure. Take I-270
    North past I-70 to Highway 367 North to Alton, IL. Drive the Great
    River Road towards Grafton. Along your way stop at some quaint
    shops and antique stores. You can stop for some homemade soup,
    breads, and desserts. In Grafton there are several very good restau-
    rants, including The Fin Inn. After the city of Grafton, stop in Pere
    Marquette State Park and Lodge (lodge- 618-786-2331). There are
    picnic areas and look-outs, with beautiful fall leaves along the drives
    in the park. Bring a picnic lunch or eat at the lodge. Then take the
    Brussels Ferry Boat across the Illinois River (cars drive right on the
    boat- free). Then follow directions and signs to the Golden Eagle
    Ferry Boat across the Mississippi River back to Missouri (this ferry
    costs about $7.00 per car). When getting off the ferry turn right on
    to Rt. B (watch for trains at crossing), then left on Rt. C to Highway
    I-70 at St. Peters, Mo, this will lead you back to St. Louis.

3. *Rombach's Pumpkin Farm* – 18639 Old Olive St. Rd., Chesterfield,
    Mo. (636) 532-7265. Take Highway 40 West to Chesterfield Airport
    Rd./Long Rd. Turn right onto Chesterfield Airport Rd. Go 1 1/2 miles
    to the Phillips 66 Gas Station, and make a left onto Olive St. Rd. It is
    a 1/2 mile down on the right side. Kids love this place — pumpkins
    everywhere! A very large display of pumpkin people, and Halloween
    decorated pumpkins, and an Old West fort for the kids to explore.
    You can choose your pumpkin from the fields or from a pile. Great
    background to take Halloween pictures of the kids. They also sell
    apple cider, apple butter, Indian corn, and gourds. Well worth the
    drive. Large groups need reservations. Open 9:00 am. to 6:00 pm. 7
    days a week during season.

4. *Halloween Fun at Grant's Farm* – 10501 Gravois Rd. (314) 843-
    1700. Kids 12 years old and younger can dress up in costumes and
    enjoy many activities including a moonlight train ride through Deer
    Park, animal shows, Halloween "Mad Science", DJ's spinning spooky
    music and photos. Thurs., Fri., and Sat.'s from 6 to 10 pm. mid-Oct.
    to Halloween. Free admission; parking is $20 per car.

5. *Thies Pumpkin Farm* – 4215 N. Hanley Rd. Corner of Hanley and
    I-70. 314-428-9878. 3120 Creve Coeur Mill Rd. 314-469-7559 Its
    Pumpkin Land! corn maze, swings, haywagon rides, live animals

and lots of pumpkins. Open around the first week in October until Halloween; Monday through Saturday 9:00 am. - 6:00 pm. Sunday 10:00 am. - 4:00 pm. Children $5.25; Adults $3.50.

6. ***Stuckmeyer's Farm*** – 249 Schneider Dr., Fenton (highway 141 and Highway 21, between Fenton and Arnold) (636) 349-1225. Family fun in Fall with pumpkins, farm animals, hayrides, pony rides, fruits and vegetables, mums and much more. Every Sat. and Sun. in October from 9:00 a.m. - 5:00 p.m.

7. ***Eckert's Pumpkin Patch*** – Three farm locations: Belleville, Grafton, Millstadt, Il. (see directions under Apple Picking). (618) 233-0513. Open daily for pumpkin patch picking beginning Oct. 1. Hours are 9:00 am. to 6 pm. You can take a wagon ride to the fields and pick your own or pick one from a large display. Plus there is a country store with apple cider, applebutter, caramel apples, Indian corn, plus large seasonal dispays and pony rides. All farms feature a Kids' Corral including a petting farm, maze, spooky area, Halloween displays, playhouses, and tractor playground. Additional activities are available on the weekends. Grafton Orchard features a Haunted Hayride the last two weekends in October.

8. ***Purina Farms*** – Gray Summit, Mo. 982-3232. Take I-44 west past Six Flags to gray Summit exit and go north (right) 2 blocks on Highway 100. Turn left on County Rd. MM (there will be a small Purina farms sign) and go 1 mile to Purina Farms entrance on the left. The last 2 week-ends in October in the evenings only is the Haunted Hayloft especially designed for the younger children. Halloween fun with games, magic show, storytelling, and Halloween cartoons are admission free, but reservations are required. Parking is $5.00 per car.

9. ***Boo at the Zoo*** – Forest Park - 781-0900. The weekend before Halloween the Zoo puts on a special display associated with Halloween. There is also a Halloween party with animal characters, snacks and a parade with children in costume. Free. call Zoo for day and time.

10. ***Magic House*** – 516 S. Kirkwood Rd., Kirkwood - 822-8900. They have several Halloween special programs for the children; make your own masks, and trick or treat day. Call for days and hours.

11. ***Faust Park*** – Highway 40 west to Clarkson / Olive. Turn right on Olive and the park is a few miles on the left. (636) 532-1030.

Halloween fun with a hayride and Trick or Treating on the carousel ride. Call for dates and times.

12. *Six Flags* – I-44 in Eureka, Mo. (636) 938-5300. They have built a ghost town for the weekends before Halloween. There is a jack-o-lantern 18 stories tall, a haunted train, palm readers, and a haunted house. Call for days, time, and cost.

13. *Hayrides* – About $125 to $150 for a group.

(a) *Greensfelder Park* – I-44 west to Allenton Rd. (314) 615-4386.

(b) *Queeny Park* – 550 Weidman Rd. - Manchester Rd. west and right onto Weidman Rd. (636) 391-0922.

(c) *Brookdale Farms* – 8004 Twin Rivers Rd. Eureka, MO 636-938-1005

My Additions to Seasonal Events

Birthday Parties

BIRTHDAY PARTIES

1. *McDonald's Restaurants* – Some of the McDonald's have a special Birthday Package available. You can have your meal, cake, and open presents in a reserved section. Please make arrangements about 2 weeks ahead. You would have to call the McDonald's near you to find out if they have this service. I do know the Kirkwood McDonald's (350 S. Kirkwood Rd.- 966-3335) has parties.

2. *Burger King Restaurants* – Some Burger Kings have special Birthday areas. A nice location is 10734 Sunset Plaza, Sunset Hills, around the intersection of Lindbergh and Watson Rd. They also have an outdoor playground. 965-2902. Call the Burger King in your area to see if they have parties.

3. *Chuck E. Cheese's Pizza* – 720 South County Center Way - 487-7317; 2669 Bogey Rd., St. Charles - 946-3444; 2805 Target Dr. (270 and Halls Ferry Rd.) -741-8001; 15913 Manchester Rd., Ellisville - (636) 391-2391. They have a Birthday Package for $10.99 per person which includes pizza, soda, cake, plates, hats, balloons, and 16 game tokens. Minimum of 6 children, and need about 2 weeks for reservations.

4. *Dierbergs School of Cooking Birthday Parties* – Clarkson- (636) 394-9504; Creve Coeur- 432-6505; St. Charles- (636) 669-0049; Southroads- 849-3698. $175.00 for 1 1/2 hours for up to 17 children age 7 and older in the kitchen of Dierbergs School of Cooking. You have your choice of a Birthday Menu, which the children prepare, plus a packet of recipes to take home, party games and prize, cupcakes, ice cream, birthday napkins, and candles. $150.00 for a 1-hour party for 5 and 6 year olds.

5. *Sisters Tea House* – 505 Main St., Fenton, MO (636) 305-1319. Open Tues.–Sat. 11:00 a.m.- 2:30 p.m. This is a wonderful luncheon tea restaurant and they also have birthday parties for young girls here. For either $13.00 per child or $16.00 per child (depending on whether or not a party host is needed to help you) the children can have time in a dress-up room with hats, dresses, gloves, boas, make-up and jewelry. They then go all dressed up to their tea party with china plates, tea cups (with strawberry lemonade) and have lunch and dessert. Please call for reservations.

6. *Tropicana Lanes Bowling* – 7960 Clayton Rd. 781-0282. For $9.95 per child, a Birthday Package includes 1 game of bowling, shoes,

soda, fries, and a hot dog. The birthday child gets a birthday bowling pin. There are serveral other packages available. There are rooms available for cake and presents. Parties can be arranged in the afternoons 7 days a week. Please call for reservations.

7. **Crestwood Bowl** – 9822 Watson Rd., Crestwood. 966-4377. Birthday Package is available for $9.00 per person which includes 1 game of bowling, shoes, hot dog, chips, and soda. $5.00 per person for game and shoes only. Parties are afternoons 7 days a week. Please call for reservations.

8. **Show Me Lanes Bowling** – 4575 Lemay Ferry. 894-8010. For $7.00 per person a birthday package includes 1 game of bowling, shoes, hot dog, fries, bowling pass, and an autograph bowling pin for the birthday child's friends to sign. Please call for days and reservations.

9. **Brunswick Lakeside Lanes** – 1254 Dougherty Ferry Rd., Valley Park. (636) 225-2400. They have regular bowling, computer bowling with different games, or bumper bowling birthday packages. Bumper bowling is great fun for the little ones - no gutter balls! The package is $13.99 each, minimum of 8 children, which includes bowling for 1 hour, shoes, ball, soft drink, pizza, paper products and bowling pin. Parties can be arranged certain times of the day, 7 days a week. Please call for reservations. Cosmic Bowling with glow in the dark bowling, lasers, fog, and rock music! It is usually late Fri. night or Sat. afternoons. Call for hours and prices.

10. **Rollercade Rollerskating Rink** – 11703 Concord Village Plaza - 842-3845. Take Lindbergh south and turn right onto Baptist Church Rd. and its 1 block down. They have a Birthday Package for $90.00 for 12 kids or less which includes admission, skates, and soda. Bring your own cake. Parties are usually Saturday, Sunday afternoons. Reservations 1 to 2 weeks ahead needed.

11. **Skateport Plaza** – 408 Weidman Rd., Ballwin. (636) 227-2800. Public sessions, roller hockey, or roller skating is available here. Birthday party packages are available for $80.00-110.00 which includes up to 10 children, their admission, skate rental, party room set up with all paper products, pizza and soda. You provide the cake. Please call for reservations.

12. **Jamestown Sports Complex** – 5105 N. Highway 67, Florissant. 355-5363. A sports complex that offers seasonal outdoor roller hockey, volleyball, and swimming, and indoor soccer, softball, and karate. A

Birthday party package is available for $100.00 which includes 1 hour of field time, party room, soda, and cupcakes for up to 15 children.

13. **Rock Roll-Orena** – 4153 Jeffco Blvd., Arnold.- (636) 464-5688. Take I-270 South to I-55 South and get off at Richardson Rd. At stop sign turn left on Highway 61 - 67 which is also Jeffco Blvd. They have a Birthday Package $110.00, depending on the day and time for up to 10 kids. Package includes admission, skates, ice cream and soda; plus a ride on the Skate Wagon. They have special party invitations for you to give out. Please call 2 weeks ahead for reservations.

14. **Ice skating party at Queeny Park** – 550 Weidman Rd., Ballwin. (636) 391-0900. (See PARKS for directions.) Have an ice skating birthday party. Skating is available during public sessions. Call for times and prices.

15. **Ice skating party at South County Recreation Center** – 6050 Wells Rd., 894-3088. (See PARKS for directions.) An ice skating birthday party can be arranged during regular skating sessions. Call for times and prices.

16. **Parties at the YMCA** – Webster YMCA- call 962-YMCA; Kirkwood YMCA- Call 965-YMCA. You can rent the pool for $95.00 per hour, usually Saturdays and Sundays after 4:30 pm. when the pool is closed to the public. The Webster YMCA has separate rooms where you can have cake and presents first, then swim the rest of the time. Please call 2 weeks ahead of time so they can get the life guards. You can also have a Kids-Gym party for $95.00.

17. **St. Louis Gymnastic Center** – 315 Pacific, Webster. 968-9494. Rent the Gymnastic Center for $137.00 for the first 10 children and $9.00 for each additional child. For 45 min. a coach will instruct the children in gymnastics. Then you can bring your own treats or cake and have a 45 min. party. Parties available on Saturday afternoons. Call for times and reservations.

18. **Robins Pony Express** – (636) 452-3737. For about $195.00 depending on location, you can have 2 ponies with saddles come to your house, or 1 pony with saddle and 1 pony with a cart. For an additional fee they will bring a petting zoo that consists of baby rabbits, goats, and hens. Please make reservaitons weeks ahead. www.robinsponyexpress.com

19. **The Clowns** – (636) 978-8716. For $115.00 for about 1 hour, the clown will do magic, make animal balloons or face painting, tell stories, and the birthday child helps the clown. There is a live rabbit in the act which the children love.

20. **Jo Jo the Clown** – 576-9628. Jo Jo will perform magic acts and puppet shows geared to involve 3 to 7 year olds in the action. Price is about $65.00, which includes treats.

21. **John Sonnenschein's (Son-In-Shine) Magic Act Zippy the Magician** – (636) 461-2031. Your children will be delighted and amazed by his tricks and magic! Objects will magically disappear and reappear right before your eyes! For around 45 mins. to an hour John will thoroughly entertain your birthday party, scouting event, or other events.

22. **Magic House** – 516 Kirkwood Rd.- 822-8900. Birthday parties are $15.00 a child and a min. of 10 to 20 children and as many as 10 adults, but at least 1 adult for each 5 children. Price includes Magic House for 1 hour and use of the party room and refreshments. Call for reservations several months in advance.

23. **Concord Soccer and Multi-Sports Club** – 12320 Old Tesson Rd. 842-3153. (I-270 and Tesson Ferry Rd.) Have a birthday party at an indoor soccer field! A Birthday party package is available starting at $125.00 which includes 45 minutes of field time, a party room, 4 pitchers of soda and cups. You bring the cake and the kids!

24. **Painted Zebra** – 10907 Manchester Rd., Kirkwood. 965-2262. A great new idea, have a ceramic painting party! A party package is $5.00, per person, plus the cost of the ceramic bisque ware. They supply the paint, glazes, brushes, stencils, and all other supplies needed and a cool place to have it! The children design and paint their own piece. It is then fired in the kiln and ready to be picked up in a few days. They can also supply decorations and cake or you can bring your own.

25. **American Girl Doll Store** – 2020 Chesterfield Mall, Chesterfield. (877) 247-5223. A very special birthday party for girls and their dolls. Call to make reservations.

26. **Professional Storyteller** – Karen Young. (636) 227-6478. She enthralls and entertains children with her original faerie tales, Native American legends, folk tales, and tales from around the world. A

"magical" 45 mins. of storytelling to preschoolers through elementary age is $100. Available for school, scout, and church functions.

27. **Spunky Beans The Clown** – Donna Wiles – (636) 928-7170. Spunky Beans can delight you with magic, ballon animals, face painting and just plain clowning around! She can perform for birthday parties, preschools, grand openings and all occasions. Call for availability and prices.

28. **Family Golfplex** – 3717 Tree Court Industrial Blvd. (In Kirkwood, off Marshal Rd.) (636) 861-2500. 18-hole miniature golf course with waterfalls, fountains, and castles! Birthday party packages available for $9.50 a child which includes golf game, hot dog, chips, and soda.

29. **Everyday circus** – 645-4445. Bring a clown or a whole circus to your house! You can have it small or you can have the works! Entertainment includes a clown, stiltwalker, balloons, fortune teller, face painting, moon bounce, pony rides, popcorn, animals, and many more options. Parties start at $150.00. Parties also available at city museum.

30. **Wanna Kick? Karate Parties** © – 8738 Rear Watson Rd., Crestwood. (1/2 mile east of Crestwood Plaza at Grant Rd.) 849-6660. For Birthdays or special events call Steve Robinson to schedule an action packed demonstration.

31. **Hammer's Food and Fun.** – 5254 S. Lindbergh. (314) 842-0700. 4103 N. Cloverleaf Dr., St. Peters. Hours are Sun. - Thurs. 11:00 am - 9:00 pm. Fri. - Sat. 11:00 am - 10:00 pm. Go-Karts, mini-golf, mini-bowling, bumper cars, and video games. Match that with pizza, pasta, salads, and desserts and you have a party! For $15.99 plus tax per person, with a 10 child min., you get an all you can eat buffet, drinks, a $5.00 game card, party room, and the birthday child gets a balloon bouquet and party bag. The games range from $.30 to $5.00 per person.

32. **Salt 'N' Patter Puppets** – Patrica. 1-(636) 629-5788. She will entertain your child's birthday party with about a 1/2 hour puppet performance and then she'll teach the children how to make their own puppets with the supplies she brings. The kids can then have their own puppet show and something to bring home! If you mention you saw this party in this book you will get $10.00 off the price of the party. Call for prices.

34. **Planet Fun** – 5849 Suemandy Dr., St. Peters. (next to Mid Rivers Mall). (636) 397-7700 This is a play palace for kids with slides, tunnels, games and food. Mon. - Thurs. all day $4.75. Fri. after 3 p.m., Sat. and Sun. $7.50. Adults free. Birthday party packages are available starting at $129.00 for 8 children.

35. **Pump It Up** – 3691 New Town Blvd., St. Charles, MO 63301, (entrance at Fountain Lakes) 636-946-9663. The Inflatable Party Zone! Kids can bounce, slide, jump, climb and laugh on these gigantic inflatables. There are several party packages available which includes playtime and the party room for gifts and optional food choices. The kids love it! Be sure to bring socks for jumping.

36. **The Dance Academy** - 637 Big Bend, Ballwin. (636) 230-5266. Colleen Kilmer has a great idea for birthday parties! You can dance your heart away at her dance studio. Birthday parties include your choice of costume and dance lesson. This is for any age group. Parties are about 1 1/2 hours. Call for time and prices.

37. **Fashions of the Past** - Carol Ann Miller. 821-0184. She can come to your house and put on a "Girls from the Past" Birthday party for little girls 6 to 10 years old, complete with her own authentic, original vintage clothing. She can also entertain at parties by having "Storytime with Grandmother Goose" (preschool to 6 years) or at Christmas time she can be "Mrs. Claus." Call for times available and prices.

38. **St. Louis Zoo** - Forest Park - For birthday parties call 314-646-4857. The zoo has "Zooper Birthday Parties!" The parties are held in a private area just for you and your guests and include individual party cakes, apple juice, fun animal related games or crafts and live animals to see and touch. Several packages are available with birthday extra starting at $300 for up to 25 guests.

39. **Faust Park Carousel** - 15189 Olive Blvd., Chesterfield. (636) 519-9950. The St. Louis Carousel Gallery is available for parties. The rental is around $150.00 for two hours which includes unlimited carousel rides for 20 guests, and a room with table and chairs for your food and beverages. Call for hours available

40. **Cats-Paw Puppet Troupe** - (636) 278-1030 - A unique style of puppet shows that will completely entertain the children. Various themes can be chosen from ; Jungle tales, Aesop fables, Mother Goose, Animals of the Forest and more. Call for reservations and prices.

41. *Cindy's Zoo -* (636) 366-9224 - Cindy Farmer - This traveling zoo will come to your house with a llama, donkey, cow, goat, sheep, chickens, rabbits, baby camel, pig, tortoise and even a reindeer! For about $160.00 an hour you can have this petting zoo, or pony or llama rides, or a combination for around $260 an hour.

42. *Whittle Shortline Railroad -* 24 Front St. Valley Park. (636) 861-3334. (near Highway141 and Marshall Rd., and Carol House Furniture.) You can design your own train party at this miniature wooden train factory and toy store. (see Museum and Entertanment Chapter) Several options to choose from including a piñata or a 4 ft. train cake! Call for times and prices.

43. *Lolli the Clown -* Jackie Barrett, (636) 441-1369. Lolli will entertain your birthday party or other events, with face painting, balloon animals and more. Please call for prices.

44. *Little Gym -* 15425 Manchester Rd., Ballwin, (Schnucks Center) Ballwin (636) 256-4500; 434 South County Center Way, St. Louis. 314-487-1993; 639 Gravois Bluff, Fenton. 636-343-5169; 12802 Olive Blvd, Creve Couer. 314-439-1100; 7347 Mexico Rd., St. Peters. 636-970-1220; 1931 West Highway 50, Fairview Heights, IL. 618-632-6711; 1015 A. Century Drive., Edwardsville, IL. 618-656-3000 Birthday parties for up to 15 children includes 1 hour supervised gym activities and games, and 30 mins. in the party room, invitations, balloon bouquet, paper goods, juice, and T-shirt for the birthday child for $198.00 to $218.00.

45. *Adrenaline Zone & Demolition Ball -* 1875 Old Hwy 94 South, St. Charles, MO. 636-940-7700. Adrenaline Zone is for ages 7 yrs. and up that is a multi-level laser tag arena. Demolition ball is for ages 12 and up and combines hockey, football, polo, and basketball while played in bumper cars! www.DB-AZ.com

46. *Mad Science Birthday Parties -* (314) 991-8000. A "Mad Scientist" will conduct a birthday party at your home for about 1 hour. They will show you the difference between magic and science and have several hands-on Mad Science activities that the kids can participate in. They supply all the materials needed and each child will get to take a completed project home. Parties start at $195.00 for up to 15 chidren.

47. *Cravings Factory -* 636-293-3823. www.cravingsfactory.com This bakery makes wonderful custom cakes for parties and also rents out inflatable bounce houses and slides. They can cater a kid's birthday

party with snow cones, cotton candy, hotdogs and more. Serving the St. Charles County: St. Charles, St. Peters, O'Fallon, MO, Wentzville, Lake St. Louis, New Town, Cottleville, Dardenne Prairie, St. Paul, and Flint Hill.

48. **Randy Erwin** - (217) 523-0973 or 1-(866) 467-3620. Randy will delight kids with 45 mins. of cowboy folklore, legends, history, music, and trick-roping. Kids love to hear his cowboy yodeling. Call for prices:

49. **Bounce U** - (636) 532-5867. 17365 Edison Ave. Chesterfield. In Chesterfield Valley shopping center, behind Home Depot. 4403 Meramec Bottom Rd., South County. (314) 845-7529. Birthday party packages start from $210 for 2 hours for up to 25 guests. These are the very large blow up slides and jumps that kids can really bounce on! Don't forget to bring your socks!

50. **Monkey Joe's** - 9061 Watson Rd., Crestwood (corner of Grant Rd., in the same parking lot as Applebee's) (314) 962-5637. Open Mon. - Sat. 10:00 am - 6:00 pm.; Sun. 11:00 am - 6:00 pm. This is a cute indoor play center for the younger ones with inflatable slides and jumps. There are many party packages to choose from. This is also available for open play time.

51. **Olympiad Gymnastics** - Many locations. Chesterfield - (636) 532-6909; Manchester - (636) 227-7460; Florissant - (314) 831-5440; St. Peters - (636) 970-1800; Ellisville - (636) 230-9496; Festus - (636) 933-0044. Several party packages are available, starting around $145.00 for 10 children, with 1 hour of gymnastic-related fun activi- ties, a medal for each child attending and a birthday trophy for the birthday child. Parties can be for the young or older child. Party room and treats can be added to a package. A great time for all.

52. **My Gym** - 15931 Manchester Rd. Ellisville. (636) 386-8496. This is a fun party for your little one with games, organized activities, rides, puppets and the use of the gym. All parties are supervised by the staff and their goal is that everyone has fun! Parties start for around $185.00 for up to 20 children for 2 hours. Call for times available.

My Additions to
Birthday Parties

My Additions to
Birthday Parties

Restaurants

RESTAURANTS

I decided to add this chapter after having a very pleasant experience at a restaurant with my children. It felt good to eat somewhere other than a fast food place and have the kids enjoy it. So this is a list of restaurants that parents will enjoy that also cater to the children.

1. **Bob Evans** – 5 locations in the St. Louis area. Great casual family restaurant, good food and good prices. Children get special place mats to color and crayons and stickers. Children's menu has lots of choices for breakfast, lunch, and dinner.

2. **Cusanelli's** – 705 Lemay Ferry Rd., 631-7686. Well known Italian restaurant for the entire family. Children's portions of pasta available.

3. **Fuddruckers** – 10752 Sunset Hills Plaza (Lindbergh and Watson Rd.) 966-3833. Very Casual with many kinds of hamburgers that include "The Works Bar". There are steaks for the heartier appetite. Special kids' meals with smaller portions and prices are available that include a free cookie from the bakery counter. Kids 12 and under can eat free, Mon. - Thurs. after 4 pm. with each adult meal purchased.

4. **Max & Erma's** – 10 Meadows Circle Dr., Lake St. Louis (636) 278-1614; 2024 MidRivers Mall, St. Peters (636) 970-1900; 79 West County Center, Des Peres (314) 965-5200. Delicious food for adults and children. Large menu selection with special kids menu. Kids can make their own ice cream sundaes for just $1.29. You can also order your dessert of chocolate chip cookies that will be baking while you are enjoying your meal!

5. **Cheeburger Cheeburger** – 2012 Chesterfield Mall, Chesterfield. (636) 532-3210; 13311 Manchester Rd., Des Peres, *next to Trader Joe's.* (314) 821-9900. Everyone loves cheeseburgers!

6. **International House of Pancakes** – 3 locations around the St. Louis area. Family restaurant that serves breakfast any time of the day! It also has good lunches and dinners. Special kids' menu with lots of choices. A favorite is the "funny face pancake", a large chocolate chip pancake with whipped cream and cherry eyes, nose and mouth!

7. **Missouri Botanical Garden Restaurant** – 4344 Shaw, 577-5100. Cafeteria style restaurant, with good salads and sandwiches for lunch. Children's sandwiches include hot dogs and peanut butter and jelly.

8. *The Old Spaghetti Factory* – 727 N. 1st, downtown in Laclede's Landing, 621-0276 – 17384 Chesterfield Airport Rd. (636) 536-9522. Full of old time atmosphere, a place parents and kids will both enjoy. Delicious pasta dinners and a special children's portion of pasta, salad, and bread. Children's menu turns into a trolley car for them to play with.

9. *St. Louis Zoo's Painted Giraffe Café* – Inside the new Living World building at the St. Louis Zoo, in Forest Park, 781-0900. Buffet dining for breakfast and lunch with a picturesque view of the zoo. Lots of choices of sandwiches and salads but they still have the kids favorite hot dogs and hamburgers.

10. *Pasta House* – Many different locations in the St. Louis area. A great Italian restaurant with a special activity menu and children's portions of pastas and salads.

11. *Red Lobster* – 6 locations in the St. Louis area. Delicious seafood at good prices. Children are welcome with a special children's menu that includes flounder, shrimp, fish platter, hamburgers and chicken fingers.

12. *Cici's Pizza* – Many locations.9745 Manchester Rd., Rock Hill, (314) 963-7200. Open Sun.–Thu. 11:00 a.m. to 10:00 p.m.; Fri.–Sat. 11:00 a.m. to 11:00 p.m. This is a great all-you-can-eat buffet pizza, pasta, salad, and dessert restaurant for $4.99 a person. Kids 3 and under eat free. The pizzas are hot and ready to eat and delicious!

13. *Applebee's.* – Many locations through out the city. A nice family atmosphere and good food. Kids eat for $2.99 and up from the kids menu, and includes beverage, ice cream sundae, and a ballon.

14. *Krieger's Pub and Grill.* – Many locations around the city. Choose from sandwiches, salads, burgers, pizza, pasta and more! Tuesday is Family night. With each paying adult, kids eat free! The kid's meal is served on a Frisbee and the soda's are in a sports bottle.

15. *Fitz's.* – 6605 Delmar Blvd., University City, The Loop. 726-9555. A unique restaurant where parents and kids can both get their favorite foods. Fitz's is also a root-beer bottling plant and this process can sometimes be seen through the glass wall that separates the plant from the restaurant. Call ahead for the bottling schedule. So of course, the menu has a variety of root-beers and floats! Also included are appetizers, salads, burgers, sandwiches, pizza, pastas, and

steaks. There is a children's menu ($3.00 to $3.50) which includes burgers, hot dogs, cheese sandwich, and spaghetti.

16. *Johnny Rockets* – 1155 St. Louis Galleria Mall. (314) 863-5533. This is an All-American hamburger diner complete with hand-dipped milkshakes and nickel jukeboxes on the tables. Great food and great atmosphere.

17. *Hard Rock Café* – 450 St. Louis Union Station. 621-7625. If the kids like music, this is the place to be! Music memorabilia is all over the walls and ceiling. There are at least 5 different children's meals to choose from for kids 10 and under for around $5.00. Don't forget that Hard Rock Café T-shirt!

18. *Blueberry Hill* – 6504 Delmar, in The Loop. (314) 727-0880. Open 7 days a week at 11:00 a.m. This is a great restaurant and fun for the older kids, especially during the day. The food is wonderful and the kids can play with the inlaid board games in the booth tops, the photo booth and sticker station, the video games and look at all the pop culture memorabilia collections, including the Simpsons and Toy Story collections. When you are done eating you can walk outside on the sidewalks and see the stars' names along the Walk of Fame. (See Museum and Entertainment Chapter.)

19. *Café Manhattan* – 511 S. hanley at Wydown, Clayton. (314) 863-5695; 992 Lin-Ferry at tesson Fery (314) 849-4143. This is a 1950's malt shop type restaurant, with counter top and barstools or tables. Great menu of pizza, salads, burgers, sandwiches, shakes, and more.

20. *Red Robin Gourmet Burgers and Spirits* – 17308 Chesterfiled Airport Rd., Chesterfield. (636) 733-0066; 120 Gravois Bluffs Circle, Fenton; 13001 Manchester Rd. (636) 305-9440, Des Peres, (314) 821-6400. This restaurant caters to kids and adults! There are TV videos, video games, great burgers, and shakes for the kids, and also seafood, ribs, and cocktails for the adults.

INDEX

Places We Liked the Best

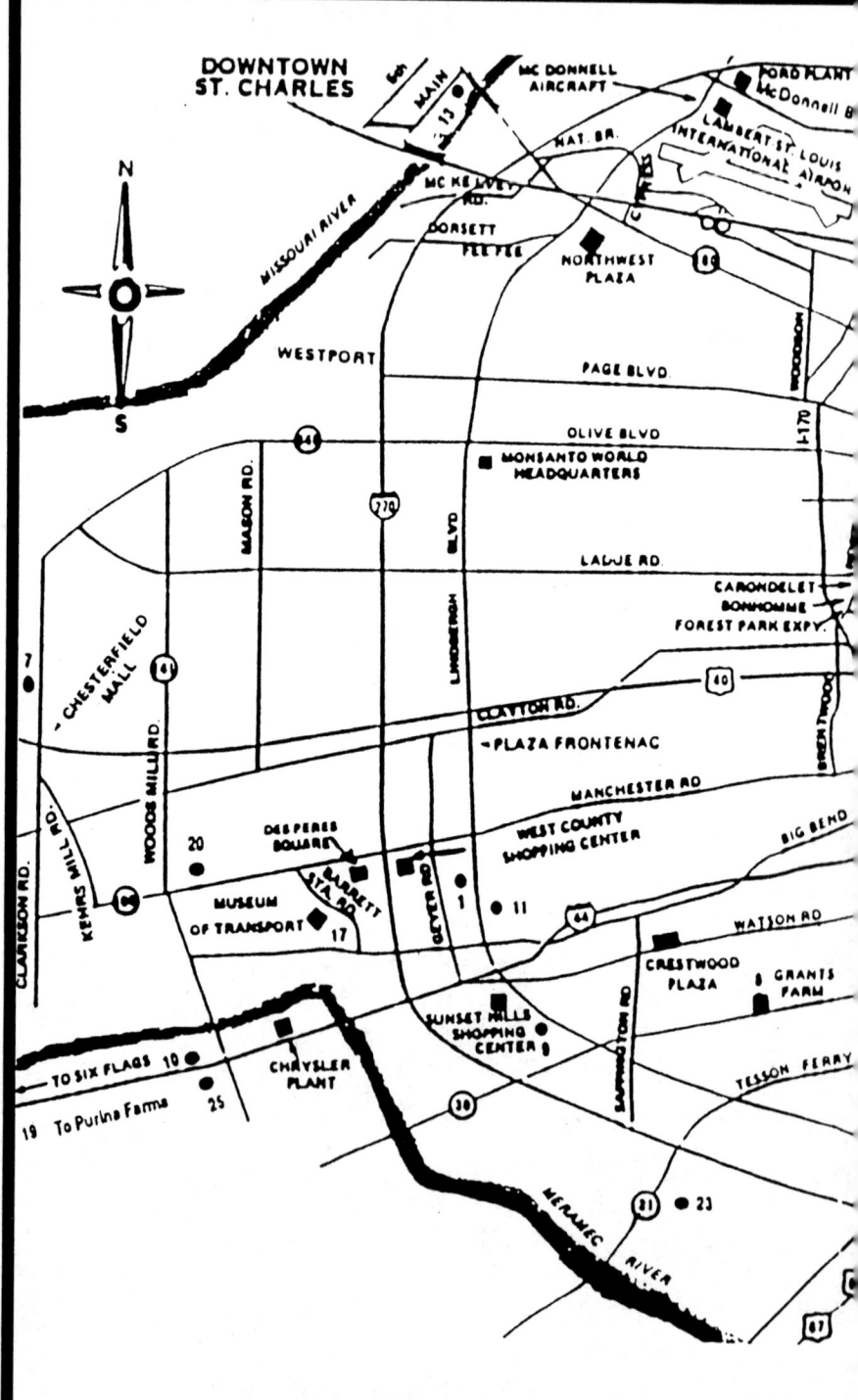

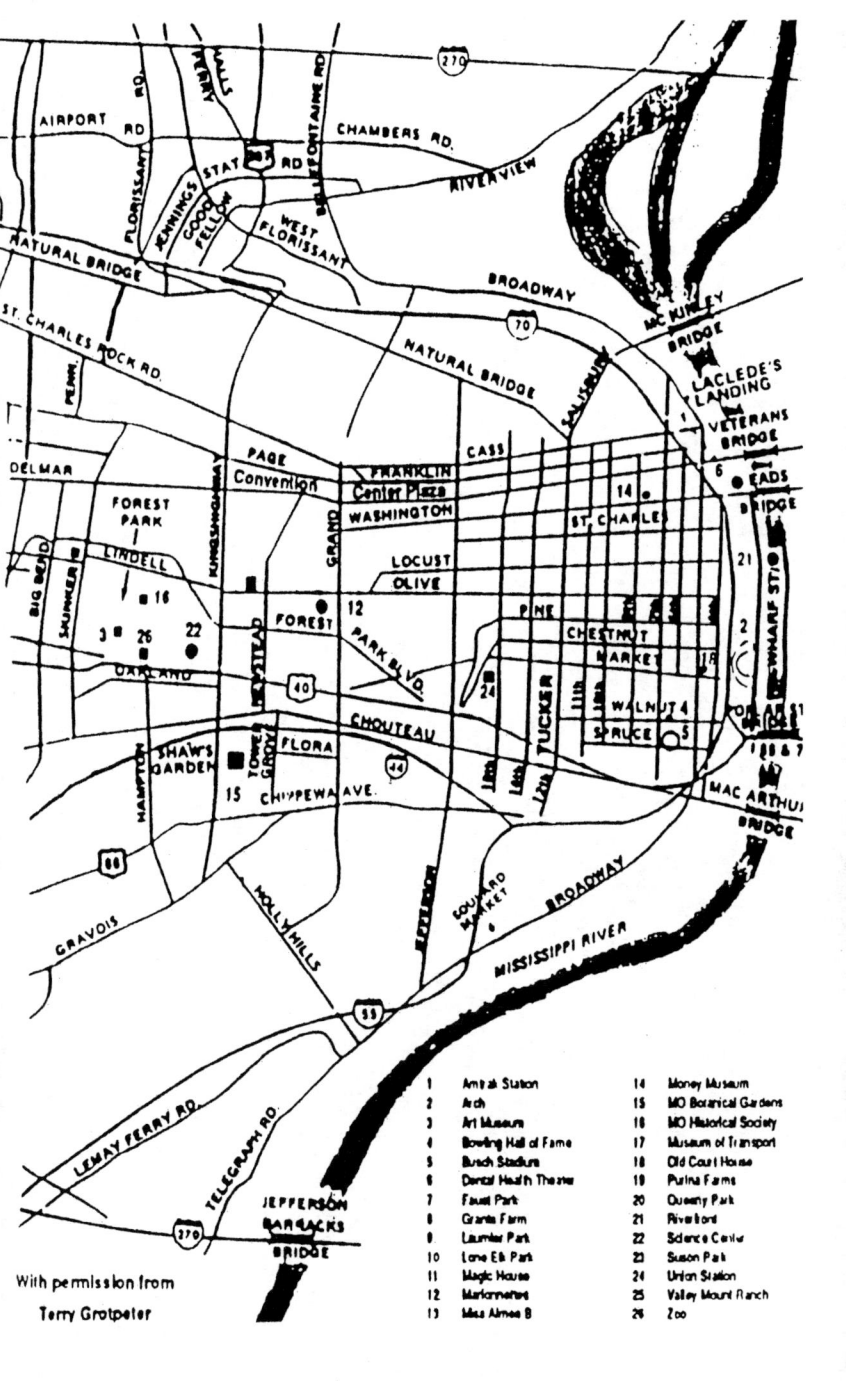

1	Amtrak Station
2	Arch
3	Art Museum
4	Bowling Hall of Fame
5	Busch Stadium
6	Dental Health Theatre
7	Faust Park
8	Grants Farm
9	Laumier Park
10	Lone Elk Park
11	Magic House
12	Marionettes
13	Miss Aimee B
14	Money Museum
15	MO Botanical Gardens
16	MO Historical Society
17	Museum of Transport
18	Old Court House
19	Purina Farms
20	Queeny Park
21	Riverfront
22	Science Center
23	Suson Park
24	Union Station
25	Valley Mount Ranch
26	Zoo

With permission from

Terry Grotpeter